AF539891

SCIENTIFIC ANALOGY OF FRUITS

By

Dr. Laxminarayan Hegde

Associate Professor
M & APs and Associate Dean
College of Horticulture, Sirsi
(Uttar Kannada dist.)
Karnataka (India)

DISCOVERY PUBLISHING HOUSE PVT. LTD.
NEW DELHI-110 002

Published by:

Tilak Wasan

DISCOVERY PUBLISHING HOUSE PVT. LTD.

4383/4B, Ansari Road, Darya Ganj

New Delhi-110 002 (India)

Phone : +91-11-23279245, 43596064-65

Fax : +91-11-23253475

E-mail : parul.wasan@gmail.com
discoverypublishinghouse@gmail.com

web : www.discoverypublishinggroup.com

***First Edition:* 2014**

ISBN: 978-93-5056-434-9

Scientific Analogy of Fruits

Printed at:

Dynamic Printers

Delhi

Preface

A fruit is generally a fleshy seed associated part of a particular plant; it is naturally and mostly edible and sweet in the raw state. By and large each and everyone in this world love fruit, though there are exceptions, we still will have a majority of folks who love fruits. It is something which has both taste and nutrients.

Fruits are good source of vitamins and minerals and are a readily available source. A fruit will boost you instantly. It is something which can quench your thirst and satisfy your hunger at the same time. Fruits are guardian angels for all the busy bees out there, who have no time to even have their breakfast. Since its handy they can be eaten even on the move.

You might have tasted fruits in your life, at least once for sure. And now if you want to taste it in a different way, then trust me, you have reached the right destination already and its none other than our own fruitsinfo.com, which is the only website dedicated to fruits, which gives you each and every possible information and daily updates on fruits.

When it comes to the uses of fruits, it is never-ending! Fruits are consumed as food by millions of people in the form of salads, soups, juices, jams and pickles.

Fruits give you all the essential nutrients and are rich in vitamins like C and A. If you need interesting tips, recipes and many more then visit this section right away! We hope that this site would prove to be the best for fruit lovers and those who like experimenting with them.

Fruits, goldmine of vitamins, minerals and fibre are ideal to consume at least 4-5 servings in a day. Since they are in the natural form, account for largest part of water and 100 per cent bad cholesterol free, it's much easier for the body to process and absorb the vitamins and minerals from the fresh fruit.

—Author

Contents

Preface

1. **Introduction** 1

Nutritional and Health Benefits of Citrus Fruits; The Nutrient Content and Functions of Citrus; Carbohydrate; Vitamin C; Folate; Potassium; Phytochemicals; Phytochemicals in Citrus Fruits; Prevention Potential of Citrus; Cardiovascular Disease; Cancer; Neural Tube Defects; Anaemia; Cataracts; Bone Metabolism and Osteoporosis; Kidney Stone Disease; Cognitive Function; Asthma; Factors Affecting Citrus Consumption; Conclusion

2. **Different Kinds of Fruits Source of Vitamins** 11

3. **Apple, Acai, Apricot, Almond, Avocado** 18

Apple; Acai; Acai Health Benefits; Acai Berry Facts; Apricot; Benefits of Apricot; Constipation; Digestion; Eyes/Vision; Fever; Skin Disease; Kidney Stones; Ashtma Problem; Respiratory Disease; Diarrhoea; Almond; Avocado; Health Benefits; Wide-Ranging Anti-Inflammatory Benefits; Optimized Absorption of Carotenoids; Supports Cardiovascular Health; Promotes Blood Sugar Regulation; Anti-Cancer Benefits

4. **Berry Fruits** 32
Cloudberry; Bilberry; Blueberry; Gooseberry; Mulberry; Raspberry; Wineberry; Huckleberry; Barberris; Nannyberry; Cranberry; Consume of Cranberries; Cancer and Heart Attack; Gallstone; Blood Thinners

5. **Banana** 40
Cavendish; Storage and Transport; Flower; Leaves; Trunk; Nutrition and Research; Other Uses

6. **Clementines, Cherry** 51
Clementine; Cherry; Nutritional Value

7. **Date, Durian** 58
Date; Durian; Nutritional Value per 100 g (3.5 oz)

8. **Figs** 71
Weight Loss; Lower Cholesterol; Coronary Heart Disease; Colon Cancer; Menopausal Breast Cancer; Diabetes; Hypertension; Sexual Weakness; Piles

9. **Grape, Grape Fruit, Guava Fruit** 76
Grape; Seed Constituents; Grapefruit; Nutritional Information; Guava Fruit; Potential Medical Uses

10. **Jackfruit** 89

11. **Kumquat, Kiwifruit** 93
Kumquat; Round Kumquat; Oval Kumquat; Characteristics; Cultivation; Jiangsu Kumquat; Hong Kong or Chin Chu; Marumi or Round Kumquat; Meiwa or Large Round Kumquat; Nordmann Seedless Kumquat; Nagami or Oval Kumquat; Kiwifruit; Heart and Colon Health; Age Related Muscular Degeneration (ARMD); Cardiovascular Disease; Constipation

12. **Lemon, Lime (Fruit), Lychee** 104
Lemon; Growing Lemons; Differences Between Orange and Lemon; Bonnie Brae; Bush Lemon Tree; Eureka; Lisbon; Ponderosa; Variegated Pink; Verna;

Villafranca; Non Culinary Uses; Commercial Use; Household Use; Insecticide; Science Education; Lemon Alternatives; Lemongrass; Cancer; Diabetic; Fights Infection; Weight Loss; Eliminates Winter Blues; Cholestrol Cleanse; Biliousness; Diptheria; Rheumatism; Scurvy; Lime (Fruit); Health Effects; Scurvy; Skin Care; Constipation; Peptic Ulcer and Respiratory Disorder; Gout; Gums; Piles; Toothaches; Lychee; Cancer; Heart Diseases; Gastro-Intestinal Troubles; Fight Infection; Prevent Blindness; Cold and Diet; Skin Protection; Pain

13. Mandarin, Mango, Purple Mangosteen, Mulberry **122**
Mandarin; Biological Characteristics; Health Benefits; Mango; Digestion; Cancer Hazards and Lower Cholestrol; Digestion; Cures Anemia and Helps in Pregnancy; Cures Acne; Brain Health; Body Immunity; Rheumatism; Scurvy; Purple Mangosteen; Mulberry; Uses in Folk Medicine; Mulberry; Parkinson Disease; Obesity; Gout; Parasitic Infections; Kidney Stones; Blood Tonic; Liver and Lung; Pain; Chemotherapy Interference; Skin Cancer; Diabetes; Pregnancy/Lactation

14. Orange, Olive **136**
Orange; Products made from Oranges; Olive

15. Passion Fruit, Papaya, Peaches, Pear, Persimmon, Pineapple, Plum, Pomegranate, Pomelo **143**
Passion Fruit; Papaya; Protection Against Heart Disease; Colon Cancer; Anti-Inflammatory Effects; Immune Support; Rheumatoid Arthritis; Promote Lung Health; Prevent Prostate Cancer; Digestive Process; Relieve Nausea; Lung Protection; Cure Dengue Fever; Skin Treatment; Peaches; Health Benefits of Peaches; Pear; Health Benefits; Nutritional Value per 100 g (3.5 oz); Cardiovascular and Colonhealth; Post-menopausal Breast Cancer; Macular Degeneration; Cancer; Constipation;

Shortness of Breath; Persimmon; Pineapple; Macular Degeration; Bone Strength; Gums Healthy; Arthritis; Hypertension; Lose Weight; Plum; Pomegranate; In Ayurvedic Medicine; Nutrients and Phytochemicals; Phenolic Content; Potential Health Benefits; Pomelo

16. Rambutan, Raisins 176
Rambutan; Nutritional Value per Serving; Health Benefits of Rambutan; Raisins; Nutritive value per 100 g of Rambutan; Mouth Problem; Bone Problem; Eye Care; Cancer; Anemia; Constipation

17. Manilkara Zapota (*Chiku*) 182
Synonyms; Other Names

18. Tomatoes, Tamarillo 185
Tomatoes; Tamarillo

19. Watermelon, Walnuts 188
Watermelon; Selecting Watermelon; Walnuts

Bibliography 193

Index 195

CHAPTER 1

Introduction

A fruit is generally a fleshy seed associated part of a particular plant; it is naturally and mostly edible and sweet in the raw state. By and large each and everyone in this world love fruit, though there are exceptions, we still will have a majority of folks who love fruits. It is something which has both taste and nutrients.

Fruits are good source of vitamins and minerals and are a readily available source. A fruit will boost you instantly. It is something which can quench your thirst and satisfy your hunger at the same time. Fruits are guardian angels for all the busy bees out there, who have no time to even have their breakfast. Since its handy they can be eaten even on the move.

You might have tasted fruits in your life, at least once for sure. And now if you want to taste it in a different way, then trust me, you have reached the right destination already and its none other than our own fruitsinfo.com, which is the only website dedicated to fruits, which gives you each and every possible information and daily updates on fruits.

When it comes to the uses of fruits, it is never-ending! Fruits are consumed as food by millions of people in the form of salads, soups, juices, jams and pickles.

Fruits give you all the essential nutrients and are rich in vitamins like C and A. If you need interesting tips, recipes and many more then visit this section right away! We hope that this site would prove to be the best for fruit lovers and those who like experimenting with them.

Fruits, goldmine of vitamins, minerals and fibre are ideal to consume at least 4-5 servings in a day. Since they are in the natural form, account for largest part of water and 100 per cent bad cholesterol free, it's much easier for the body to process and absorb the vitamins and minerals from the fresh fruit.

Nutritional and Health Benefits of Citrus Fruits

Citrus fruits have long been valued as part of a nutritious and tasty diet. The flavours provided by citrus are among the most preferred in the world, and it is increasingly evident that citrus not only tastes good, but is also good for people. It is well established that citrus and citrus products are a rich source of vitamins, minerals and dietary fibre (non-starch polysaccharides) that are essential for normal growth and development and overall nutritional well-being. However, it is now beginning to be appreciated that these and other biologically active, non-nutrient compounds found in citrus and other plants (phytochemicals) can also help to reduce the risk of many chronic diseases. Where appropriate, dietary guidelines and recommendations that encourage the consumption of citrus fruit and their products can lead to widespread nutritional benefits across the population.

The Nutrient Content and Functions of Citrus

Citrus is most commonly thought of as a good source of vitamin C. However, like most other whole foods, citrus fruits also contain an impressive list of other essential nutrients, including both glycaemic and non-glycaemic carbohydrate (sugars and fibre), potassium, folate, calcium, thiamin, niacin, vitamin B_6, phosphorus, magnesium, copper, riboflavin, pantothenic acid and a variety of phytochemicals. In addition, citrus contains no fat or sodium and, being a plant food, no cholesterol. The average energy value of fresh citrus is also low, which can be very important for consumers concerned about putting on excess body weight. For example a medium orange contains 60 to 80 kcal, a grapefruit 90 kcal and a tablespoon (15 ml) of lemon juice only 4 kcal.

Carbohydrate

The main energy-yielding nutrient in citrus is carbohydrate; citrus contains the simple carbohydrates (sugars) fructose, glucose and sucrose, as well as citric acid which can also provide a small amount of energy. Citrus fruits also contain non-starch polysaccharides (NSP), commonly known as dietary fibre, which is a complex carbohydrate with important health benefits. The predominant type of fibre in citrus is pectin, making up 65 to 70 percent of the total fibre. The remaining fibre is in the form of cellulose, hemicellulose and trace amounts of gums. Citrus also contains lignin, a fibre-like component. In the body, NSP holds water-soluble nutrients in a gel matrix which delays gastric emptying and slows digestion and absorption. This tends to promote satiety, and may reduce the rate of glucose uptake following consumption of glycaemic (available) carbohydrate, thus helping to prevent a surge in blood glucose levels. Improper regulation of blood glucose results in either hyperglycaemia (high blood glucose) or hypoglycaemia (low blood glucose). NSP can also interfere with the reabsorption of bile acids which may help in lowering plasma cholesterol levels.

A reasonable goal for dietary NSP/fibre intake is 25 to 30 g/day, but in many developed countries the actual average intake is closer to 15 g. With one medium orange containing approximately 3.0 g of NSP, citrus fruit can make a valuable contribution to meeting the daily fibre goal.

Vitamin C

Vitamin C (ascorbic acid), an essential water-soluble vitamin, plays a key role in the formation of collagen, a primary component of much of the connective tissue in the body. Adequate collagen synthesis is essential for strong ligaments, tendons, dentin, skin, blood vessels and bones, and for wound healing and tissue repair. The weakening of these tissues is a symptom of vitamin C deficiency. Vitamin C is an important aid in the absorption of inorganic iron; it has also been shown to aid in the treatment of anaemia and stress. Contrary to popular belief, vitamin C does not seem to prevent the onset of the common cold, but in some studies it has been reported to reduce the length and severity of the symptoms.

Contemporary interest in vitamin C centres on its ability to perform antioxidant functions. As an antioxidant, it can help prevent the cell damage done by "free radical" molecules as they oxidize protein, fatty acids and deoxyribonucleic acid (DNA) in the body. Free radical damage has been implicated in the progression of several diverse and important disease states including cancer, cardiovascular disease and cataract formation. Being a good source of antioxidants, if regularly consumed, citrus can be an important part of a diet aimed at reducing the risk of such chronic disease.

Only 10 mg of vitamin C per day are required to prevent vitamin C deficiency and the devastating disease scurvy. However, for good health and sufficient body storage of vitamin C, 30 to 100 mg/day is generally recommended, although some recent studies have provided evidence that more than 200 mg/day may be optimal for the prevention of chronic disease. Too much vitamin C (above 500 mg), generally seen with very high levels of supplementation, may be dangerous, especially for those at risk of iron overload. Consuming five servings of fruits and vegetables each day can result in an intake of about 200 mg of vitamin C. Citrus fruits are a particularly good source of vitamin C, with one medium orange or grapefruit providing approximately 70 mg and 56 mg, respectively. A 225 ml glass of orange juice contains approximately 125 mg of vitamin C.

Folate

Folate is a water-soluble vitamin essential for new cell production and growth. It helps in the production of DNA and ribonucleic acid (RNA) and mature red blood cells, which ultimately prevent anaemia. In the United States, the recommended daily intake of folate is 180 mcg for females and 200 mcg for males. Over the past decade, however, it has become clear that higher levels of folic, 400 mcg, are associated with the prevention of neural tube defects, a severe birth defect (Centres for Disease Control and Prevention, 1992). A 225 ml glass of orange juice provides 75 mcg of folic acid.

Potassium

Potassium is an essential mineral that works to maintain the body's water and acid balance. As an important electrolyte, it plays a role in transmitting nerve impulses to muscles, in muscle contraction and in the maintenance of normal blood pressure. The daily requirement of potassium is approximately 2 000 mg and, while frank deficiency of potassium is rare, there is some concern that a high sodium-to-potassium intake ratio may be a risk factor for chronic disease. Increased consumption of citrus fruits and juices is a good means of increasing potassium intake. One medium orange and one 225 ml glass of orange juice provide approximately 235 mg and 500 mg of potassium, respectively.

Phytochemicals

These naturally occurring compounds found in plants have a wide range of physiological effects and may help to protect against various chronic diseases, including cancer and heart disease. The wide variety and number of known phytochemicals continue to grow, as does understanding of their role and importance in the diet. Several classes of phytochemicals, including monoterpenes, limonoids (triterpenes), flavanoids, carotenoids and hydroxycinnamic acid, have been isolated from citrus.

Phytochemicals in Citrus Fruits

The possible anticarcinogenic mechanisms of phytochemicals include their antioxidant capabilities, their effects on cell differentiation, an increased activity of the enzymes that detoxify carcinogens, an altered colonic milieu, and the blocking of nitrosamines. The regular intake of a varied mix of phytochemicals is only possible through the consumption of plant-based foods, such as citrus, as part of the normal diet.

Prevention Potential of Citrus

There is considerable evidence that citrus foods may help reduce the risk, or retard the progression, of several serious diseases and disorders.

Cardiovascular Disease

It is well accepted that a diet low in saturated fat and cholesterol and rich in fruits and vegetables reduces the risk of heart disease. Epidemiological studies have also shown a significant association between vitamin C intake and protection against cardiovascular mortality, but the precise mechanism of protection is still unclear. One major culprit in the development of heart disease appears to be a high level of oxidized low-density lipoprotein (LDL), the so-called bad cholesterol. Significantly, a recent study has shown that high intakes of vitamin C (500 mg/day) obtained from the juice of freshly squeezed oranges, prevented a rise in the levels of oxidized LDL, even in the presence of a high-saturated fat diet.

A low dietary intake of folate contributes to the decrease of plasma folate and the raising of plasma homocysteine levels. Homocysteine is a toxic agent for the vascular wall and, when plasma levels rise above normal, there is an increased risk of cardiovascular disease. An inverse dose-response relationship has been identified for fruit and vegetable intake and plasma homocysteine levels. Frequent consumption of folate-rich foods, such as oranges and orange juice, tends to increase plasma folate levels and, thus, lower homocysteine levels.

Cancer

After numerous studies of fruit and vegetable intake and cancer development, there is a consensus that consuming these foods has a protective effect. However, it is unlikely that one anticarcinogenic substance in particular is responsible for the benefit. There is reasonable scientific support for vitamin C's protective role in cancer. Many of the animal, cell culture and human studies have suggested it has a positive effect. However, epidemiological studies provide good evidence that protective effects are more closely associated with the consumption of fruits and vegetables rather than with the enormous levels of vitamin C often used in cell culture and animal studies.

Neural Tube Defects

During the first stage of pregnancy, adequate folate intake is critical for reducing the risk of severe birth defects, namely spina bifida and anencephaly. Public health recommendations in the United States include the consumption of 400 mcg of folate per day for women of child-bearing age (Centres for Disease Control and Prevention, 1992). Regular consumption of citrus foods can help supply adequate folate and thus reduce the risk of these birth defects.

Anaemia

Vitamin C can increase the absorption of non-haem iron (the inorganic iron form found in plant foods) two- to fourfold. The bioavailability of non-haem iron is much lower than that of haem iron, which is found in foods of animal origin. Vegetarians and individuals who consume little meat and animal products are at an increased risk of iron-deficiency, which can progress to anaemia over time. Worldwide, anaemia is one of the most serious nutrient-related public health problems, resulting in poor growth, impaired psychomotor development, reduced physical performance and decreased cognitive function. Consuming citrus fruits rich in vitamin C can help prevent anaemia and its devastating consequences.

Cataracts

Oxidation of the eye's lens plays a central role in the formation of age-related cataracts. The role of dietary antioxidants, such as vitamin C, in the aetiology of cataracts has been a recent focus of research. Lower cataract risk has been shown in individuals with high blood concentrations or intakes of vitamin C and carotenoids. There is now evidence to show that a high level of vitamin C intake over the long term decreases the risk of cataract development. Although epidemiological studies that measure past nutrient intake and status suggest a protective effect from citrus, further studies are needed to examine the long-term benefits of citrus fruit consumption and cataract protection.

Bone Metabolism and Osteoporosis

The influence of nutrient intake on bone density is an area of current research with many unanswered questions. Long-term intake of various foods may be important to bone health, possibly because of their beneficial effect on the acid base balance. Vitamin C intake has been associated with bone mineral density, but more work in this area is necessary to understand the mechanism of interaction.

Kidney Stone Disease

A kidney stone is a crystal structure formed by excessive salts in the urine. The most common type of stone is the calcium stone. A stone will increase in size until it is not passable and becomes lodged in the ureter. Stone symptoms include severe back pain, blood in the urine and fever. Stones strike men three to four times more often than women. Some people prone to stones have been found with insufficient levels of citrate in their urine and it has been suggested that eating citrus fruits and drinking orange juice may help prevent kidney stones by increasing urinary citrate. More research is needed in this area, but increasing fruit consumption is a nutritionally sound recommendation that may prove to be very beneficial for individuals at risk of certain kinds of kidney stones.

Cognitive Function

Elevated homocysteine levels are associated with cognitive dysfunction in the elderly. Older subjects with greater intakes of fruits and vegetables, and the corresponding nutrients vitamin C and folate, have been shown to perform better on cognitive tests. The consumption of a satisfactory diet, containing nutrient-dense foods, appears to be associated with better cognitive function in the elderly. More research is needed to determine the effect of long-term citrus consumption on cognition.

Asthma

Some studies suggest that a diet low in vitamin C is a risk factor for asthma. Vitamin C is the major antioxidant substance present in the airway surface liquid of the lungs, where it could be important in protecting against oxidants. More research is needed to understand whether vitamin C and citrus consumption is protective in the causation and progression of asthma.

Factors Affecting Citrus Consumption

In many populations, even among people who know that citrus is nutritious, the consumption of citrus is often very low. The reasons for this are varied, but it indicates that knowledge of a nutritional benefit is just one of the many factors that influence food choices. Among the other factors that greatly influence what foods people consume are: an individual's food preferences and previous experience with a given food; cultural values, perceptions, attitudes and societal influences including the media and advertising; and, most directly, the availability, taste and price of food items. For these reasons, it is difficult to bring about widespread behavioural change. Clearly, strategies are more likely to modify behaviour and improve health if they are directed towards the relevant influences and barriers. Some of the barriers to purchasing and consuming citrus are high cost, fear of harmful pesticides and quick spoilage.

Over the past two decades, rising incomes and the shift in consumer preferences towards healthier, more convenient products have contributed to a growth in demand for citrus. Income levels also influence the variety and form of citrus consumed; in developed countries more processed citrus is consumed than in developing countries where people consume more fresh citrus. Further increases in citrus consumption are possible, but will require an integrated approach to improving consumer awareness and bringing about behavioural change.

Conclusion

The health benefits associated with citrus consumption are clear . Citrus fruits are nutrient-dense foods that can be good sources of carbohydrates, including dietary fibre, and many vitamins and minerals. Citrus fruits are equally valuable among populations who need to overcome and prevent micronutrient deficiencies as well as those concerned with problems of overnutrition, obesity and diet-related chronic diseases.

As nutritionists and public health specialists learn more about the relationship between diet and health, the importance of balanced and varied dietary intakes becomes ever more evident. Accordingly, there is an increasing emphasis on promoting high levels of fruit and vegetable intakes among most population groups. Citrus consumption has a considerable potential to expand as part of this overall recommended increase in fruit and vegetable consumption.

While the supply of citrus is a problem in some areas, a greater obstacle is often the lack of effective demand for citrus. Addressing both supply and demand problems, as appropriate, will require that a range of issues, such as agriculture and trade policies, food and nutrition policies, dietary guidance and nutrition education, and marketing, are addressed effectively and in a comprehensive manner. In many countries, a multifaceted approach that brings together, as appropriate, representatives of producers, processors, importers, retailers and consumers with nutritionists and public health specialists can have a significant impact on citrus consumption. Given that increasing the consumption of citrus benefits both producers and consumers, building effective partnerships to that end should not be difficult and would be an invaluable investment in the nutritional well-being and health of the population.

CHAPTER 2

Different Kinds of Fruits Source of Vitamins

Along with vegetables, fruits are the major dietary source of vitamins A and C as well as some minerals and an excellent source of dietary fibre.

A variety of fruits is more likely to yield a wider intake of nutrients. Bananas are excellent source of pyridoxine (Vitamin B_6). Kiwi fruits are better source of ascorbic acid (Vitamin C) than citrus fruits.

Fresh fruits are fairly low in calories because they contain much water and little fat. However addition of sugar to the canned and frozen fruits increases the calories considerably. The less sugar, the fewer calories.

The improved transport and storage system have resulted in an increasing range of varieties of fruits being readily available throughout the year.

The following is a brief outline of the many fruits available to enjoy,some will have a link to a more detailed explanation that will guide you choose the right fruit for your need.

Fruit provides a dazzling array of vitamins and minerals; it contains fibre and is low-fat.

Apples - the most popular of all fruits and generally available all year round. Perfect for eating raw as a snack and an ideal for making puddings and desserts.

Apricots - delicious when ripe, provide beta carotene and a rich source of minerals and vitamin A.

Avocado - the only fruit that contains fat (monounsaturated fat). Avocados are best eaten raw, slice or add to salad.

Bananas - the best-known tropical fruit and one of the extremely nutritious and versatile fruit. Rich in potassium, riboflavin, niacin and dietary fibre, They have high energy value and good for growing children and athletes. Excellent for low-salt, low-fat and cholesterol-free diets. Hundreds of different varieties of banana flourish in the tropics from sweet yellow pygmy to large fibrous plantains and green bananas which can only be used for cooking.

Cherries - Sweet cherries can be eaten raw, stewed or in tarts and cakes. remember to buy cherries with their stings on and use any without the stem first as they don't last long. Cherries are very high in vitamin C and potassium and also contain fibre.

Custard Apples - Custard apple have thick scally skin and a soft, smooth flesh with inedible seeds. They are picked before they are fully ripe, so allow 4-5 days for firm fruit fruit to ripe. Good source of vitamin C, fibre, magnesium and potassium.

Dates - are extremely delicious, it supply significant amount of iron making them an excellent food for anaemia or chronic fatigue. They contain more natural sugar than any other fruit.

Durian - Despite the fruit's disgusting smell, when ripe the flavour of the flesh, is the most delicious of tropical fruits. The fruit is eaten fresh and chilled, scooped out using a spoon and discarding the seeds. The rich custardy flesh can be eaten just as it is or pureed to make ice cream or milk shakes. The flesh is also used for making jam and cakes and is available canned.

Fruits are nature's most bountiful and versatile creation. No other foods offer such a variety of colours, texture,scents and flavours.

Figs - oval or pear shaped, it can be eaaten fresh or dried. They are well known for their laxative and digestive properties. Their high natural sugar content makes them the sweetest of all fruits. The flavour varies, sepending on where they were grown and how ripe they are.

Grapefruits - One of the largest citrus fruit, a cross between the pomelo and the shaddock. High in vitamin C, grapefruits are best eaten raw, a traditional breakfast fruit - the best way to eat is to cut them in half and scoop out the flesh with a spoon.

Grapes - have been used in wine making for thousand of years and red wine is known to help prevent heart disease. A great energy source because of their natural fruit sugar content.

Guavas - delicious eaten raw, the whole fruit is edible an average-sized guava contains about seven times the recommended daily intake of vitamin C. Guava also provides vitamin A and is high in fibre.

Jackfruit - when unripe both seeds and the flesh are eaten as a vegetables. Ripe fruit maybe eaten on its own or added to fruit salad.

Kiwifruit - are best eaten uncooked, the easiest way to eat is to cut the fruit in half and scoop the flesh out of the skin with a spoon or you can peel and cut into cubes or slices.

Kumquat - (cumquat) the name means "golden orange" in Chinese. Kumquats are often preserved in sweet syrup and used for marmalade and garnishes, but fresh ones are delicious in fruit salads or for eating just as they are.

Lemons - rarely eaten on its own, lemons are an indispensable ingredients in the kitchen. Lemon juice can be used instead of vinegar in sauces, for seasoning in vinaigrette and as instant dressing for fish and shellfish. The best way to store lemon is in the vegetable crisper in the fridge you can put lemons in fruit bowl for a shorter, check them often - if one starts to spoil, the rest will quickly follow.

Limes - are only green because they are picked unripe but if left to ripen they turn yellow. Limes can be used like lemons but as a juice is more acidic, usually less is needed. To make the juice flow more, you can microwave the limes for 2-3 seconds before squeezing. Mostly used in drinks (lime cordials) and in cooking.

Lychees - fresh lychees are best eaten raw as a refreshing end to a meal. Simply remove the shells, then nibble or suck the flesh off the stone. Rich in Vitamin C.

Mandarins - or tangerines named after the city of Tangier in Morocco - a citrus fruit that is actually a variety of orange. Always choose deep orange to orange-red fruits, heavy for their size with birght lustre. Loose skin is normal but avoid fruits with punctures, mould soft spots or very pale skins.

Mangoes - grows in many tropical climates worldwide, The fruit ranges in colour from green to golden yellow and orange red and its flesh is a juicy, deep orange surrounding a large flat inedible stone. Mangoes also make excellent ice creams, sorbets, sauces and drinks like smoothies.

Mangosteen - contrary to its name, the mangosteen doesn't resemble or taste like the mango. It resemble like an apple-having a short stem and four thick leaf-like bracts which form a rosette encsing the brownish-purple fruit.

Nectarine - the flesh is rich, sweet and juicy and is well suited for eating fresh and for using in ice cream, pies and fruit salads. Colour ranges from silvery white or yellowy orange to pinkish red. The white-fleshed varieties are considered the best and usually the most expensive. Nectarines are often described as a cross between a peach and a plum but nectarines are actually a variety of smooth-skinned peach.

Oranges - are best eaten in their natural state but can be used in variety of desserts, pastries, fruit salads, mousses, souffles, ice creams and sorbets. They can be squeezed for juice or used to marinade poultry or fish. Oranges fall into two groups, sweet oranges which can be eaten raw and bitter oranges which cannot but are used for making marmalade, jams and jellies.

Fresh fruit makes a nutritious, low-kilojoule breakfast food or snack and often provides much needed dietrary fibre.

Passionfruit - The most popular variety is the purple passionfruit about the size of a chicken egg. it has a highly fragrant, sweet, but slightly tart, tasting fruit, can be spooned out and eaten fresh or added to fruit salad, pavlova, it makes a very popular drink, ice cream and sorbets and a flavouring for all kinds of desserts.

Papaya - or pawpaw, a large tropical fruit whose ripe flesh can be juicy, creamy, orange red or yellow. In the centre is a mass of large peppery black seeds which are edible and sometimes crushed and used as a spice. Ripe papaya is eaten as a breakfast fruit or as a dessert. it can be pureed for ice cream, sorbets and iced drinks.

Peaches - the most familiar peaches are round or "beaked" with a pointed and they are seldom sold by variety but by colour of their flesh- yellow or white. Which you choose is a matter of preference, some people believe that white peaches have the finer flavour. Peaches are delicious eaten on its own or in fruit salad.

Pears - contain a small amount of vitamin A & C and some potassium and riboflavin. pears should should always be bought when they are in perfect condition as they deteriorate quickly.

Persimmons - the fruit of a tree originally from Japan, persimmons are now widely grown in all parts of the world. Resembling a tomato in appearance, the fruit is round and smooth-skinned, changing from yellow to red when it ripens. Eat as a dessert in fruit salads, in baking or in preserves.

Pineapple - Derived from the Spanish word *'pina'* meaning pine cone. Pineapples have a juicy, sweet-but sometimes slightly tart-fragrant flavour. They are best eaten fresh, serve pineapple flesh in slices, wedges or chunks. It is also available in cans, dried and glace. A good source of vitamin C.

Plums - contains more antioxidant than any other fruit. Plums are delicate so make sure that the one you buy are unblemished and they should be plump and firm. The small sugar plum is dried to make prunes. Delicious stewed, plums are also ideal for making chutneys.

Pomegranates - an exotic looking fruit about the size of a large apple, with a thin tough skin- usually golden to deep red, filled with edible seeds in crimson pulp. To use, cut the fruit in half with a very sharp knife and scoop out the tangy sweet seeds, separate them from the white pith and eat them fresh. Can be added to salads, use as a garnish on sweet and savoury dishes or press to extract juice.

Pomelo - a small citrus tree native to tropical Asia and the tropical world. Similar to grapefruit but larger and with a very thick rind. The rind comes off readily making segmenting the fruit easy. The flesh varies from yellow to pink and it is generally sweeter and not as tart as grapefruit.

Rambutans - the fruit grows in cluster, with a deep crimson outer skin. The flesh is translucent and the pale seed is edible when young. Related to lychees and are sometimes known as "hairy lychees" (about 5 cm/2 inches in diametre) and look quite different but have a similar texture. They can be added to salads, can be made into jams or jellies but are best eaten on their own.

Sapodillas - a tropical fruit with rough, brown skin but are sweet and luscious like vanilla flavoured banana custard. Make sure the fruit is soft and thoroughly ripe as unripe flesh can be quite bitter.

Star apple - The fruits are green to purple with a smooth skin. When sliced horizontally the flesh is translucent white with the seeds forming a star shape. it is best eaten ripe, scooped straight from the skin. It is ripe when soft and should be eaten immediately, but it is still alright to refrigerate for a few days.

Strawberries - A unique fruit, the seeds grow around the outside of the fruit rather than inside it. Comes in many different sizes, colours and shapes, ranging from conical to oval or heart-shaped. Best to eat on their own or with natural yoghurt. Use in desserts, fruit salads, preserves or in milk shakes.

Tamarillos - related to tomatoes and sometimes called "tree tomatoes", they are the size of an egg tomato with dark red skin and the fruit has a strong sweet flavour suitable for both sweet or savoury dishes. It can be used in jams, chutneys and sorbets.

Watermelon - the high water content of watermelons means that they are low in calories. They contain some viatamins B and C. Watermelon is excellent juiced, chopped in fruit salad or just eaten in chunky slices.

CHAPTER 3

Apple, Acai, Apricot, Almond, Avocado

APPLE

The apple is the pomaceous fruit of the apple tree, species *Malus domestica* in the rose family Rosaceae. It is one of the most generally refined tree fruits. The tree originated from Central Asia, where its wild forebear is still found today. There are more than 7,500 known cultivars of apples ensuing in range of desired characteristics. Cultivars differ in their yield and the ultimate size of the tree, even when grown on the same rootstock.

At least 55 million tonnes ofappleswere grown worldwide in 2005, with a value of about $10 billion. China produced about 35 per cent of this total. The United States is the second leading producer, with more than 7.5 per cent of the world production. Turkey, France, Italy and Iran are among the leading apple exporters.

Apples, as eaten in the fresh state, are a healthy uplifting, crunchy snack. They quench your desire and their acid content makes them a natural mouth freshener. To bite into a fresh picked apple is a memorable experience. The juice is honey sweet and spicy tart at the same time and the flesh is fragrant and crisp.

The Greek and Roman mythology refer to apples as signs of love and beauty but Apple contain vitamins like Vitamin C,

Beta-Carotene, iron and potassium etc., The Vitamin C pleased may not be as good as Oranges but apples have very high mineral contents, pectins, malic acid which are good in normalizing the intestines. Apple is good for handling of anaemia, dysentery, heart disease, headache, eye disorders, kidney stones and promotes strength and energy. Apple juice is good to overcome a liverish feeling, further, apples are not likely to cause allergic reactions and are excellent means of providing essential fluids to the body.

ACAI

Acai Common name: Acai berry, palm berry, acai palm, jussara, cabbage palm are some of the common names in which Acai is known by

Origin: They are known to originate from Amazon rainforest in Brazil

Scientific Name: Euterpe oleracea

Appearance: Acai is a small, round, blackish purple fruit, looks alike in appearance but smaller than a grape with lesser pulp and a single big seed at the centre.

Nutrients in Acai: Acai has an amazing antioxidant quality. It is very rich in antioxidants such as Vitamin C and polyphenols. Acai also haves an ample amount of iron, calcium and vitamin A with amino acid.

Fatty acid helps in the movement and absorption of fat-soluble vitamins like A, D, E and K. Acai has high caloric values and fats when compared with other berries and fruits.

Nutritional Content (Per 100 g)

Calories	534
Carbohydrates	51.9 g
Protein	8.12 g
Total Fat	32.61 g
Calcium	260 mg
Iron	4.8 mg
Vitamin A	1002 U

Note: The content given in the table is fixed according to our calculation; hence it may not be accurate.

Healthy fats in Acai: Acai berry is very rich in healthy Omega fats. Nearly 50 per cent of the Acai berry is fat - with 74 per cent of the fat coming from healthy unsaturated fats such as:

- Omega 3
- Omega 6
- Omega 9

Nineteen different amino acids have been identified in Acai. Since amino acids are the basic building blocks of protein, over 8 grams of protein is there in every 100 gram of Acai. Acai berry is an excellent source of Plant Sterols. Three plant sterols (or photosterols) present in acai are:

- B-sitosterol
- campesterol
- sigmasterol

Photosterols have numerous health benefits for maintaining healthy heart and digestive function. Acai contain as much Vitamin C as blueberries and has over 1000 IU of Vitamin A in every 100 grams.

In addition, potassium, calcium, magnesium, copper and zinc are all found in Acai. Acai has a strong fibre profile. Around 14 grams of fibre is present in every 100 grams of freeze dried Acai powder.

Acai Health Benefits

High level antioxidants in acai promotes overall body health and fight free radicals.

- It boosts up energy levels.
- It helps to add luster to skin and nails.
- It strengthens our immune system and provides greater energy and stamina.
- It Provides better sleep and anti-allergenic support.
- It also improves digestion and sexual function.
- It Promotes better circulation and aids in preventing blood clots.

Helps in prevention and treatment of Alzheimer (brain disorder) and arteriosclerosis (stiffening of arteries).

Acai Berry Facts

- Acai palm also grows in the rainforests of South America.
- It has been used as a weight loss supplement.
- Acai berry contains plenty of omega oil substances which help to keep the blood pressure (BP) level under control.
- Acai fruit is very low in sugar content.
- Acai berry contains high levels of essential amino acids, fibre, plant sterols (controls cholesterol) and anti-oxidants.
- Acai pulp contains 10 to 30 times the anthocyanins found in red wine by equal volume.

One of the most important acai studies, conducted by the University of Florida, tells us that acai fruit has caused a "self destruct" reaction in Leukemia cells.

Antioxidants are one of the best ways to lower the chance of getting cancer and there is no other better way to get them than through acai berry juice or pills.

The fatty acid proportion of Acai looks like olive oil, which many experts believe that it might be the contributing element for the low occurrence of heart-related problems.

Fibre and Omega fatty acids are two of the biggest weapons highly used in preventing diabetes and heart diseases by lowering the blood pressure and cholesterol levels.

Acai berry is one of the most powerful anti-aging super foods. Acai fruit's anti-aging effect is a combination of high level anthocyanins and strong antioxidant vitamin content.

Acai berry is known to contain ten times as many antioxidant vitamins as grapes and twice as many as blueberries and thirty three times more antioxidant power than both red grapes and red wine.

In addition to the high levels of omega-6 and omega-9 fatty acids, acai fruit also haves a protective effect on the heart and cardiovascular system. The omega-6 and omega-9 fatty acids in acai berries play a vital role in lowering cholesterol level in the blood.

Apricot

The Apricot belongs to the family *Prunus armeniaca*, of a Species *Prunus*, classified with subgenus *Prunus*. The apricot is called as golden orange fruit due to its velvety skin and sweet, fine, smooth textured flesh is steeped in multicultural folklore. Apricot fruit has a high content of beta-carotene; beta-carotene which is found in apricots is converted to vitamin A in the body. Other Nutritional contained in fruits include apricots are vitamin C iron and fibre content.

Benefits of Apricot

Anemia

Anemia is the condition where the blood has lower concentration of red blood cells (RBCs) or RBCs having below average amount of hemoglobin. This condition is most commonly caused by iron deficiency. The presence of iron in apricot makes it an excellent food for anemia sufferers.The small but essential amount of copper in the fruit makes the iron available to the body.Liberal consumption of apricot can increase the production of hemoglobin in the body. This is ideal for women after their menstrual cycle, especially those with heavy flow.

Constipation

If you are going through constipation from long time, then having apricots on daily basis can be very beneficial.Apricots are rich in fibre and hence are good for smooth bowel movements. It is often recommended to patients who are regularly suffering from constipation due to its laxative natures.The cellulose and pectin content in apricot is a gentle laxative and are effective in the treatment of constipation.Cell membrane helps the intestine to work properly, and the latter helps in absorbing water in intestine. The pectin absorbs and retains water, thereby increasing bulk to stools, aiding in smooth bowel movement. Hence, if you suffer from chronic constipation, consume 6 to 8 apricots per day should help improve your condition.

Digestion

Apricot helps to clear your entire acidity and digestion problem. Take an apricot before meal to aid digestion, as it contains alkaline reaction in the digestive system.

Eyes/Vision

The large amount of vitamin A is essential to maintain or improve eyesight.Insufficiency of this vitamin can cause night blindness and impair sight. Apricot is highly recommended for eye because it contains Vitamin A which helps in improving vision for the person.

Fever

Apricot juice is given to the patients suffering from fever as it provides necessary vitamins, minerals, calories and water to the body. Some people also use steamed apricot during fevers. Blend some honey and apricots with some mineral water and drink to cool down fever.It quenches the thirst and eliminates the waste products effectively from your body. Tone up your eyes, stomach, liver, heart and nerves by supplying vitamins and minerals.

Skin Disease

Apricot oil is best for skin care. It quickly absorbs the skin and does not keep the skin oily when applied. Apricot not only useful for maintaining the skin smooth and shiny, also aids in treating number of skin diseases such as s Pear has fibres which not just help you avoid the hassles of constipation and regular bowel movements; it also binds the bile salts in the colon and efficiently flushes them out of your system.

Fibre lowers high cholesterol levels, people at risk for atherosclerosis or diabetic heart disease. Since bile salts are made from cholesterol, the body must break down more cholesterol to make more bile, a substance that is also necessary for digestion. The end result is a lowering of cholesterol levels.eat the pear whole for its precious fibre that is highly beneficial for your colon health.

Fibre also binds to cancer-causing chemicals in the colon, preventing them from damaging colon .This may be one reason why diets high in fibre-rich foods, such as pears, are associated with a reduced risk of colon cancer.

Person Whom May Not Consume Apricot

Kidney Stones

Person with containing calcium oxalate as kidney stones should not consume too much of this fruit, because the fresh apricots contains small amount of oxalate and hence, it will cause severe damages to the kidney.

Asthma Problem

Sulfur compounds such as sulfur dioxide are rich in dried apricots. Patients who suffer from asthma strictly must not eat this fruit as the chemical compounds present in this may causes severe reactions in your body.

Respiratory Disease

Due to Excessive intake of amygdalin present inside the apricot fruit can cause cramps, vomiting, respiratory distress and in severe cases, nervous system depression and fatal respiratory failure. So persons who suffer from respiratory and nervous disease should avoid this fruit.

Diarrhoea

Diarrhoea can be caused due to infections, antibiotics, or teething effects in children. Loose motion will occur frequently. In this case, your stool becomes watery. If you loose too much water, you might suffer from dehydration. Diarrhoea kills more children than malaria, AIDS and TB. In fact, diarrhoea is the second leading cause of death in children under 5 years of age.

ALMOND

The almond is native to Iran, from northwestern Saudi Arabia.The sweet almond itself contains practically no carbohydrates and may therefore be made into flour for cakes and cookies for low carbohydrate diets or for patients suffering from diabetes mellitus or any other form of glycosuria.

Almond flour is gluten free and therefore a popular ingredient in cookery in place of wheat flour for gluten-sensitive people, and people with wheat allergies and coeliac disease.Almonds can be processed into a milk substitute simply called almond milk; the nut's soft texture, mild flavour, and light colouring (when skinned) make for an efficient analog to dairy, and a soy-free choice, for lactose intolerant people, vegans, and so on. Raw, blanched, and lightly toasted almonds all work well for different production techniques, some of which are very similar to that of soymilk and some of which actually use no heat, resulting in "raw milk".

AVOCADO

The avocado (*Persea americana*) is a tree native to Central Mexico, classified in the flowering plant family Lauraceae along with cinnamon, camphor and bay laurel. Avocado or alligator pear also refers to the fruit (botanically a large berry that contains a single seed) of the tree.

Avocados are commercially valuable and are cultivated in tropical and Mediterranean climates throughout the world. They have a green-skinned, fleshy body that may be pear-shaped, egg-shaped, or spherical. Commercially, it ripens after harvesting. Trees are partially self-pollinating and often are propagated through grafting to maintain a predictable quality and quantity of the fruit.

P. americana, or the avocado, originated in the state of Puebla, Mexico. The native, undomesticated variety is known as a *criollo*, and is small, with dark black skin, and contains a large seed. The oldest evidence of avocado use was found in a cave located in Coxcatlán, Puebla, Mexico, that dates to around 10,000 BC. The avocado tree also has a long history of cultivation in Central and South America; a water jar shaped like an avocado, dating to AD 900, was discovered in the pre-Incan city of Chan Chan. The earliest known written account of the avocado in Europe is that of Martín Fernández de Enciso (c.1470–c.1528) in 1518 or 1519 in his book, *Suma De Geographia Que Trata De Todas Las Partidas Y Provincias Del Mundo.* The first written record in English of the use of the word 'avocado' was by Hans Sloane in a 1696 index of Jamaican plants. The plant was introduced to Indonesia in 1750, Brazil in 1809, the Levant in 1908, and South Africa and Australia in the late 19th century.

Health Benefits

Promote Heart Health

Before reviewing special health areas in which avocados truly shine in terms of their health benefits, it's worth remembering the big picture. That's exactly what Victor Fulgoni and his fellow researchers at Nutrition Impact, LLC did when they reviewed data from the federal government's National Health and Nutrition Examination Study (NHANES 2001-2006) and the dietary intake of 14,484 U.S. adults. Amazingly, only 273 adults participating in this study reported consumption of avocado within the last 24 hours. Amongst the 273 participants who reported recent consumption of avocado, however, nutrient intake was found to be significant higher than other participants for several vitamins (vitamin E and vitamin K), several minerals (potassium and magnesium), and at least one desirable macronutrient (total dietary fiber). Avocado consumers were also determined to be lower in weight and lower in body mass index than non-consumers. Total fat intake, total monounsaturated fat intake, and total polyunsaturated fat intake was higher in consumers of avocado, even though their overall calorie intake was not significantly different from non-consumers of avocado. This nationwide comparison of avocado consumers and non-consumers doesn't prove that avocado consumers get health advantages from avocado. Nor does it prove that avocado consumption makes us lower in weight. But it does point us in the general direction of viewing avocado as a health supportive food that may give us a "leg up" in terms of health and nourishment.

Wide-Ranging Anti-Inflammatory Benefits

The ability of avocado to help prevent unwanted inflammation is absolutely unquestionable in the world of health research. The term "anti-inflammatory" is a term that truly applies to this delicious food. Avocado's anti-inflammatory nutrients fall into five basic categories:

- *phytosterols*, including beta-sitosterol, stigmasterol, and campesterol;
- *carotenoid antioxidants*, including lutein, neoxanthin, neochrome, chrysanthemaxanthin, beta-cryptoxanthin, zeaxanthin, violaxanthin , beta-carotene and alpha-carotene;
- *other (non-carotenoid) antioxidants*, including the flavonoids epicatechin and epigallocatechin 3-0-gallate, vitamins C and E, and the minerals manganese, selenium, and zinc;
- *omega-3 fatty acids*, in the form of alpha-linolenic acid (approximately 160 milligrams per cup of sliced avocado); and
- *polyhydroxylated fatty alcohols (PSAs)*.

Arthritis—including both osteoarthritis and rheumatoid arthritis—are health problems that have received special research attention with respect to dietary intake of avocado. All categories of anti-inflammatory nutrients listed above are likely to be involved in avocado's ability to help prevent osteoarthritis and rheumatoid arthritis. One especially interesting prevention mechanism, however, appear to involve avocado's phytosterols (stigmasterol, campesterol, and beta-sitosterol) and the prevention of too much pro-inflammatory PGE2 (prostaglandin E2) synthesis by the connective tissue.

Optimized Absorption of Carotenoids

No single category of nutrients in avocado is more impressive than carotenoids. Here's a list that summarizes key carotenoid antioxidants provided by avocado:

- alpha-carotene
- beta-carotene

- beta-cryptoxanthin
- chrysanthemaxanthin
- lutein
- neochrome
- neoxanthin
- violaxanthin
- zeaxanthin

Optimal absorption of these fat-soluble phytonutrients requires just the right amount and combination of dietary fats—and that is exactly the combination that is provided by avocado! Included within avocado are generous amounts of oleic acid, a monounsaturated fatty acid that makes it easier for the digestive tract to form transport molecules (chylomicrons) that can carry carotenoids up into the body. This great match between avocado's fat content and its carotenoids also extends to the relationship between avocado and other foods. Consider, for example, a simple salad composed of romaine lettuce, spinach, and carrots. This simple salad is rich in carotenoids, and when we eat it, we definitely get important carotenoid benefits. But recent research has shown that if one cup of avocado (150 grams) is added to this salad, absorption of carotenoids will be increased by 200-400 per cent! This improvement in carotenoid absorption has also been shown in the case of salsa made with and without avocado. (That's even more reason, we think, to try our recipe for 15-Minute Halibut with Avocado Salsa!)

Supports Cardiovascular Health

Avocado's support for heart and blood vessels might be surprising to some people who think about avocado as too high in fat for heart health. From a research standpoint, however, many metabolic aspects of heart health - including levels of inflammatory risk factors, levels of oxidative risk factors, and blood fat levels (including level of total cholesterol) - are improved by avocado. In addition, we know that heart health is improved by intake of oleic acid (the primary fatty acid in avocado) and by intake of omega-3 fatty acids (provided by avocado in the form of alpha-linolenic acid and in the amount of 160 milligrams per cup). Since elevated levels of homocysteine form a key risk factor for heart disease, and since B vitamins are very important for healthy regulation of homocysteine levels, avocado's significant amounts of vitamin B-6 and folic acid provide another channel of heart support.

Research on avocado and heart disease remains in the preliminary stage, with studies mostly limited to lab studies on cells or animals fed avocado extracts. But we fully expect to see large-scale human studies confirming the heart health benefits of this unique food.

Promotes Blood Sugar Regulation

One of the most fascinating areas of avocado research—and one that may turn out to be the most unique for health support—involves carbohydrates and blood sugar regulation. Avocado is relatively low-carb food, with about 19 per cent of its calories coming from carbs. It's also a low-sugar food, containing less than 2 grams of total sugar per cup, and falls very low on the glycemic index. At the same time, one cup of avocado provides about 7-8 grams of dietary fiber, making it an important dietary source of this blood sugar-regulating nutrient. Given this overall carb profile, we would not expect avocado to be a problematic food for blood sugar unless it was eaten in excessive amounts (many cups per serving).

Within its relatively small carb content, however, avocado boasts some of the most unusual carb components in any food. When it is still on the tree, avocado contains about 60 per cent of its carbs in the form of 7-carbon sugars. In sizable amounts, 7-carbon sugars (like mannoheptulose, the primary carb in unripened avocado) are rarely seen in foods. Because of their rare status, food scientists have been especially interested in the 7-carbon sugars (mannoheptulose, sedoheptulose, and related sugar alcohols like perseitol) found in avocado. The 7-carbon sugars like mannoheptulase may help regulate the way that blood sugar (glucose) is metabolized by blocking activity of an enzyme called *hexokinase* and changing the level of activity through a metabolic pathway called glycolysis. Research in this area is still a long way from determining potential health benefits for humans from dietary intake of these 7-carbon sugars. But it's an exciting area of potential health benefit for avocado, especially since this food is already recognized as low glycemic index.

One final interesting observation comes from this research on avocado and its carbs: after five days of ripening (post-harvest, beginning with removal of the avocado from the tree), the carb profile of avocado changes significantly. The 7-carbon sugars change from being the predominant form of carbs in avocado (60%) to being an important but minority component (between 40-50% of total carbs). With ripening, the 5-carbon sugars—especially sucrose—become the predominant carbs. While it's too early in the research process to draw health-oriented conclusions from this information, these findings may be encouraging us to consider degree of avocado ripeness as an important factor in its health benefits. We already know to stay away from an extremely overripe avocado that has become overly soft and has developed dark sunken spots on its skin. Perhaps off in the future, we'll be able to zero in on exact amounts of avocado ripeness that offers different types of unique health benefits, including carb-related benefits.

Anti-Cancer Benefits

The ability of avocado to help prevent the occurrence of cancers in the mouth, skin, and prostate gland has been studied in a preliminary way by health researchers, mostly through the use of lab studies on cancer cells or lab studies involving animals and their consumption of avocado extracts. But even though this anti-cancer research has been limited with respect to humans and diet, we believe that the preliminary results are impressive. The anti-cancer properties of avocado are definitely related to its unusual mix of anti-inflammatory and antioxidant nutrients. That relationship is to be expected since cancer risk factors almost always include excessive inflammation (related to lack of anti-inflammatory nutrients) and oxidative stress (related to lack of antioxidants). But here is where the avocado story gets especially interesting. In healthy cells, avocado works to improve inflammatory and oxidative stress levels. But in cancer cells, avocado works to increase oxidative stress and shift the cancer cells over into a programmed cell death cycle (apoptosis), lessening the cancer cell numbers. In other words, avocado appears to selectively push cancer cells "over the brink" in terms of oxidative stress and increase their likelihood of dying, while at the same time actively supporting the health of non-cancerous cells by increasing their supply antioxidant and anti-inflammatory nutrients. We look forward to large-scale studies in this area involving humans and dietary consumption of avocado.

CHAPTER 4

Berry Fruits

A berry fruit generally refers to any small fruit that lacks seeds and can be eaten whole.

The blackberry is the most extensively available fruit.

The shrub produces a bramble fruit and it grows to an height of 3 m which are used in desserts, wine and jams.

It is best for growing at fast rates in scrub, woods and hill sides. This fruit can spread widely.

It can tolerate poor soil conditions and it captivates places like wasteland and building sites easily.

The leaves are palmate with three to five leaflets with flowers of pink or while.

The flowers appear from May to August that ripens to dark purple or black fruit, forming the "blackberry".

It is actually not a berry, but it is an aggregate fruitof numerous drupelets.

Cloudberry

Cloudberry is a pale red fruit that grows to a height of 25 cm,initially which turns into amber colour in autumn.

When cloudberry ripes it acquires soft, juicy, golden-yellow and are rich in Vitamin C.

It is a good supplement to cure scurvy due to its rich Vitamin C content.

It acts as an inbuilt natural preservative due to a good content of benzoic acid.

The Cloudberry leaves can cure problems like urinary tract infections as used in the ancient Scandinavian herbal medicine.

In Sweden, they are also used as an ice cream topping.In Canada, cloudberries are used to flavor a special beer.

Bilberry

Bilberry is a name given to species of low-growing shrubs of the genus Vaccinium (family Ericaceae) that bear tasty fruits.

This species also known as blaeberry, whortleberry, whinberry, myrtle blueberry, and other names regionally.

Bilberries are rarely cultivated but fruits are sometimes collected from wild plants growing on public lands, especially in Scandinavia and Poland.

Vaccinium uliginosum fruit is odon in Swedish and juolukka in Finnish.The fruits are eaten fresh, or are usually made into jams, juices or pies.

Bilberry fruit contains high concentrations of tannins, that act as both an anti-inflammatory and an astringent.

Bilberry fruit offer relief for vascular disorders such as capillary weakness, venous insufficiency, and hemorrhoids.

Blueberry

Blueberry refers to the plants of genus Vaccinium, which also includes cranberries, bilberries, and many wild shrubs

This plant produces edible, round, blue berries (botanically false berries) with flared "crowns" at the end.

In North America, the most common cultivated species is *V. corymbosum*, the Northern Highbush Blueberry.

These plant can be both cultivated as well as picked wild.The fruit are first white, then reddish-purple, and turn blue on ripening. These are used in jellies, jams & pies.

Improves antioxidant in body systems and hence provides special protection from oxidative stress and helps in the protection of cardiovascular system.

Large number of phytonutrients are found in blueberries.This helps to resist the diseases towards the body.

Gooseberry

The gooseberry is a well-known fruit-bush that are found in northern and central Europe and in North America.

Gooseberries grow best in summer humid, cool regions with great winterchilling.

The fruit are borne singly or in pairs at the axils, is a berry with many minute seeds at the centre.

Gooseberry is a bush, that grows upto a height of 1-3 m.

The branches are thick with sharp spines, standing out singly of two or three from the bases of the lateral leaf shoots.

A gooseberry may be green, white, yellow, or shades of red from pink to purple to almost black.

This fruit contains more than 80 per cent of water. It also has protein, carbohydrate, fibre, minerals and vitamins. It also contains Gallic acid which is a potent polyphenol.

Mulberry

This used as both fruit and ornament the mulberry should be more generally planted.

Even if the fruit is not to the taste, the tree is naturally open-centreed and round-headed, and is an interesting subject.

The fruits are in great demand by the birds, and after they begin to ripen the strawberry beds and cherry trees are freed from robins and other fruit-eating birds.

Mulberry refers both to the mulberry tree and to the fruit of that tree.

The mulberries are small to medium-sized trees native to warm temperate areas of Asia and North America.

They are fast-growing when young, but soon become slow-growing and rarely exceed 10-15 m tall.

The leaves are alternately arranged, simple, often lobed, more often lobed on juvenile shoots than on mature trees, and toothed on the margin.

The fruit is a multiple fruit, 2-3 cm long, red ripening dark purple.

The fruit is an edible fruit and is widely used in some places.

Raspberry

The Raspberry is not a true berry, but it is a composite fruit.It has the capacity of widely spreading.

It is also known as Red Raspberry which is a tart and sweet fruit.

It is similar to blackberry but it is different in size and colour.It plants in l ate summer or the early autumn.

Raspberry grows in a place like forests or fields especially where there is free space due to fire or wood-cutting processes that has occurred.

A golden Raspberry, which is in pale yellow, has been selected by horticulturalists.

Another raspberry called black raspberry which is known as blackcap, is a North American species. It is a cultivar of Rubus occidentals.

Wineberry

Wineberry (*Rubus phoenicolasius*), is also known as Japanese Wineberry, that are orange or red in colour around 1cm in diameter.

This fruit is mainly used for making wine, despite the name, they are not fit for making wines (they taste tart).

These are found extensively in the eastern part of the United States and Europe and are prevalent in New Zealand.

The moist and loamy soil supports their growth widely, with protection from the wind.

This plant bears fruit in the summer or in the early autumn.

The fruit is orange or red in colour with a diameter of around 1cm. The leaves are whitish underneath.

Huckleberry

Huckleberry is a name used in North America for several plants in two closely related genera in the family Ericaceae, Gaylussacia and Vaccinium.

Fruits are edible, sweet, and grows to an height of 10 mm in diameter, that are mostly borne singly.

Leaves of this plant are used for tea during the winter.

Huckleberry is rich in antioxidants and is used as a culinary fruit in herbal medicinal preparations.

Huckleberry supplements may keep your heart healthy by improving blood flow to the heart.

This also helps to keep your blood vessels strong and may reduce your risk of developing atherosclerosis.

This beneficial activity of Huckleberry is mainly due to components called anthocyanins.

Barberris

Barberris belongs to the genus of about 450-500 species of deciduous and evergreen shrubs from 1-5 m tall with thorny shoots.

The native of this fruit is the temperate and subtropical regions of Europe, Asia, Africa, North America and South America.

The deciduous species are noted for good autumn colour, the leaves turning pink or red before falling.

This fruit contain a chemical called berberine, is used to inhibit the growth of bacteria in test tubes, and hence helps to promotes the function of good immune system.

The barberry fruit extract appear to have natural antihistamine and anti-allergy potential.

It has been used in Indian folk medicine to treat diseases like diarrhea, fever and improves appetite, relieve upset stomach, etc.

Nannyberry

Nannyberry is a large shrub or small tree native to the north-eastern United States and southern Canada.

The Nannyberry is also called as Sweet viburnum or Sheepberry.

Like all viburnums, the leaf of the Nannyberry is oppositely arranged on the twig.

The leaf of this fruit is oval in shape, with 3.5 inches long, finely serrate, with a winged petiole.

The flowers are small, whitish and arranged in large round clusters.

The fruit is a small round blue-black drupe, about 3/8 of an inch on a reddish stem.

The leaves of this fruit , as well as the concoctions made from the seeds, berries, and bark, are used to treat the problems such as respiratory, digestive and menstrual problems as well as relieve pain and relieve anxiety.

Cranberry

Cranberries are low, creeping shrubs or vines up to 2 metres long and 5 to 20 centimetres (2 to 8 in) in height; they have slender, wiry stems that are not thickly woody and have small leaves.

The flowers are dark pink, with very distinct *reflexedpetal,* leaving the style and stamens fully exposed and pointing forward. They are pollinated by bees. The fruit is a berry that is larger than the leaves of the plant; it is initially white, but turns a deep red when fully ripe. It is edible, with an acidic taste that can overwhelm its sweetness.

Since the early 21st century within the global functional foodindustry, raw cranberries have been marketed as a "super fruit"due to their nutrient content

Consume of Cranberries

Bacterial Disease

Cranberry are known to protect against bladder infections by preventing bacteria from sticking to the bladder wall.

cranberries also protect the stomach from ulcer-causing bacteria and protect the lining of the gastrointestinal (GI) tract, promoting GI health. Cranberries have also been shown to protect against cancer and heart disease.

Cancer and Heart Attack

While we often think of cranberries as an ingredient in cranberry sauce or fall and winter baked goods, you can eat fresh, raw cranberries. Cranberries have numerous health benefits, including a high concentration of antioxidants. Use of raw cranberries in a variety of foods is to add a tart, fresh flavor to salads, relishes and other dishes.so it helps to protect against cancer and heart diseases.

Gallstone

It is a pear shaped pouch that is located on the underside of the right portion of the liver. It can hold 45 milliliters of bile at a time. Gallstones are hard object that forms in the gall bladder, cyctic duct, hepatic duct or bile duct . It is irregular in shape, and is usually about a size of a marble, and could be much larger. It varies in colour from yellow, black or red.

Gallstone composed of calcium salt, phospholipids, lecithin, bilirubin (a pigment), bacteria and crystallized cholesterol. These products are filtered through the liver and accumulate in the gall bladder. Drink a lot of water with cranberry fruit juice and/or aloe vera juice.

This is good to reduce inflammation and will help expel the tiny stones toward the intestine. Person prone to gallstone are advised to have a diet low in fat and cholesterol. Eat food with a lot of fibre, fibre stimulate the digestive function and in turn produce more bile juice which help to remove the stones from the intestine.

Person Whom May Not Consume Cranberries

Blood Thinners

The formation of blood clots in your arteries and veins, which reduces your risk of having a heart attack or stroke. Blood thinners are most often prescribed to individuals with an abnormal heart beat — referred to as atrial fibrillation — or people who have had heart valve surgery or individuals with congenital heart defects.It san be classified into two categories, anticoagulants and antiplatelets.

Anticoagulants include medications such as warfarin and heparin, and work by lengthening the time it takes your blood to clot by interfering with the chemical reaction. Antiplatelets include aspirin, which work by preventing platelets from clumping together to form clots. Photo Credit Jupiterimages/ liquidlibrary/Getty Images

If you have blood vessel or heart disease, or if your blood flow is poor, your doctor may recommend you take blood thinners. When prescribed new medication, it is important to talk to your doctor about possible food interactions with the medication. The salicylates and vitamin K in cranberry can affect the way certain blood thinners work. One medium apple with contains almost 4 grams of dietary fibre.

CHAPTER 5

Banana

Banana is the common name for herbaceous plants of the genus *Musa* and for the fruit they produce. Bananas come in a variety of sizes and colours when ripe, including yellow, purple, and red.

Almost all modern edible parthenocarpic bananas come from two wild species – *Musa acuminata* and *Musa balbisiana*. The scientific names of bananas are *Musa acuminata*, *Musa balbisiana* or hybrids *Musa acuminata* × *balbisiana*, depending on their genomic constitution. The old scientific names *Musa sapientum* and *Musa paradisiaca* are no longer used.

Banana is also used to describe Enset and Fe'i bananas, neither of which belong to the aforementioned species. Enset bananas belong to the genus *Ensete* while the taxonomy of Fe'i-type cultivars is uncertain.

In popular culture and commerce, "banana" usually refers to soft, sweet "dessert" bananas. By contrast, *Musa* cultivars with firmer, starchier fruit are called plantains or "cooking bananas". The distinction is purely arbitrary and the terms "plantain" and "banana" are sometimes interchangeable depending on their usage.

They are native to tropical South and Southeast Asia, and are likely to have been first domesticated in Papua New Guinea. Today, they are cultivated throughout the tropics.

They are grown in at least 107 countries, primarily for their fruit, and to a lesser extent to make fibre, banana wine and as ornamental plants.

The banana plant is the largest herbaceous flowering plant. The plants are normally tall and fairly sturdy and are often mistaken for trees, but their main or upright stem is actually a pseudostem that grows 6 to 7.6 metres (20 to 24.9 ft) tall, growing from a corm. Each pseudostem can produce a single bunch of bananas. After fruiting, the pseudostem dies, but offshoots may develop from the base of the plant. Many varieties of bananas are perennial.

The structure of bananas looks like a long curving cylinder. The bottom end is narrowed to a point and the top end has a thick stem that attaches the fruit to the inflorescence stalk. A small group of bananas is referred as "hands". Many hands are collectively called as "bunches". Banana has smooth and thick skin and often has a few vertical ridges that run along the length of the fruit. The flesh of the fruit is in creamy white and soft.

The fruit, which is technically referred as berry, changes from deep green to yellow or red, and the length ranges from 2-½ to 12 inches and 3/4 to 2 inches. The flesh, ivory-white to yellow or salmon-yellow, may be firm, astringent, even gummy with latex when unripe, turning tender and slippery, or soft and mellow or rather dry and mealy or starchy when ripe. The flavor may be mild and sweet or subacid with a distinct apple tone. The common cultivated types are generally seedless with just vestiges of ovules visible as brown specks. Occasionally, cross-pollination with wild types will result in a number of seeds in a normally seedless variety.

Leaves are spirally arranged and may grow 2.7 metres (8.9 ft) long and 60 cm (2.0 ft) wide. They are easily torn by the wind, resulting in the familiar frond look.

Each pseudostem normally produces a single inflorescence, also known as the *banana heart*. (More are sometimes produced; an exceptional plant in the Philippines produced five.) The inflorescence contains many bracts (sometimes incorrectly called petals) between rows of flowers. The female flowers (which can develop into fruit) appear in rows further up the stem from the rows of male flowers. The ovary is inferior, meaning that the tiny petals and other flower parts appear at the tip of the ovary.

The banana fruits develop from the banana heart, in a large hanging cluster, made up of tiers (called *hands*), with up to 20 fruit to a tier. The hanging cluster is known as a bunch, comprising 3-20 tiers, or commercially as a "banana stem", and can weigh from 30-50 kilograms (66-110 lb). In common usage, *bunch* applies to part of a tier containing 3-10 adjacent fruits.

Individual banana fruits (commonly known as a banana or 'finger') average 125 grams (0.28 lb), of which approximately 75 per cent is water and 25 per cent dry matter. There is a protective outer layer (a peel or skin) with numerous long, thin strings (the phloem bundles), which run lengthwise between the skin and the edible inner portion. The inner part of the common yellow dessert variety splits easily lengthwise into three sections that correspond to the inner portions of the three carpels.

The fruit has been described as a "leathery berry". In cultivated varieties, the seeds are diminished nearly to non-existence; their remnants are tiny black specks in the interior of the fruit.

Bananas are naturally slightly radioactive, more so than most other fruits, because of their high potassium content, and the small amounts of the isotope potassium-40 found in naturally occurring potassium. Proponents of nuclear power sometimes refer to the banana equivalent dose of radiation to support their arguments.

The genus *Musa* is in the family Musaceae. The APG II system, of 2003 (unchanged from 1998), assigns Musaceae to the order Zingiberales in the clade commelinids in the monocotyledonous flowering plants. Some sources assert that the banana's genus, *Musa*, is named for Antonius Musa, physician to the Emperor Augustus. Others say that Linnaeus, who named the genus in 1750, simply adapted an Arabic word for banana, *mauz*. The word *banana* itself might have come from the Arabic *banan*, which means "finger", or perhaps from Wolof *banaana*. The genus contains many species; several produce edible fruit, while others are cultivated as ornamentals.

Banana classification has long been a problematic issue for taxonomists due to the way Linnaeus originally classified bananas as two species based only on their methods of consumption, *Musa sapientum* for dessert bananas and *Musa paradisiaca* for plantains. However, this simplistic classification has proved to be inadequate to address the sheer number of cultivars (many of them synonymous) existing in its primary centre of diversity, Southeast Asia.

Ernest Cheesman first discovered that *Musa sapientum* and *Musa paradisiaca*, described by Linnaeus, were actually cultivars and descendants of two wild and seedy species, *Musa acuminata* and *Musa balbisiana*, both first described by Luigi Aloysius Colla. He recommended their abolition in favour of reclassifying bananas according to three morphologically distinct cultivars – those primarily exhibiting the botanical characteristics of *Musa balbisiana*, those primarily exhibiting the botanical characteristics of *Musa acuminata*, and those with characteristics that are the combination of the two.

Researchers Norman Simmonds and Ken Shepherd proposed the genome-based nomenclature system in 1955. This system eliminated almost all the difficulties and inconsistencies of the nomenclature system of bananas based on *Musa sapientum* and *Musa paradisiaca*. Despite this, *Musa paradisiaca* is still recognized by some authorities today, leading to confusion.

Generally, modern classifications of banana cultivars follow Simmonds' and Shepherd's system. The accepted names for bananas are *Musa acuminata*, *Musa balbisiana* or *Musa acuminata* × *balbisiana*, depending on their genetic ancestry.

Synonyms include:

- *Musa × sapientum* L.
- *Musa paradisiaca* L.
- *Musa × paradisiaca* L.
- *Musa paradisiaca* L. subsp. *Musa sapientum* J. G. Baker
- *Musa rosacea* N.J. von Jacquin
- *Musa violacea* J.G. Baker
- *Musa cliffortiana* L.
- *Musa dacca* P.F. Horaninow
- *Musa rosacea* N.J. von Jacquin
- *Musa × paradisiaca* L. subsp. *sapientum* (L.) C.E.O. Kuntze
- *Musa × paradisiaca* var. *dacca* (P.F. Horaninow) J.G. Baker *ex* K.M. Schumann

All widely cultivated bananas today descend from the two wild bananas *Musa acuminata* and *Musa balbisiana*. While the original wild bananas contained large seeds, diploid or polyploid cultivars (some being hybrids) with tiny seeds are preferred for human raw fruit consumption. These are propagated asexually from offshoots. The plant is allowed to produce two shoots at a time; a larger one for immediate fruiting and a smaller "sucker" or "follower" to produce fruit in 6–8 months. The life of a banana plantation is 25 years or longer, during which time the individual stools or planting sites may move slightly from their original positions as lateral rhizome formation dictates.

Cultivated bananas are *parthenocarpic*, which makes them sterile and unable to produce viable seeds. Lacking seeds, propagation typically involves farmers removing and transplanting part of the underground stem (called a corm). Usually this is done by carefully removing a sucker (a vertical shoot that develops from the base of the banana pseudostem) with some roots intact. However, small sympodial corms, representing not yet elongated suckers, are easier to transplant and can be left out of the ground for up to two weeks; they require minimal care and can be shipped in bulk.

It is not necessary to include the corm or root structure to propagate bananas; severed suckers without root material can be propagated in damp sand, although this takes somewhat longer.

In some countries, commercial propagation occurs by means of tissue culture. This method is preferred since it ensures disease-free planting material. When using vegetative parts such as suckers for propagation, there is a risk of transmitting diseases (especially the devastating Panama disease).

As a non-seasonal crop, bananas are available fresh year-round.

Cavendish

In global commerce, by far the most important cultivars belong to the triploid AAA group of *Musa acuminata*, commonly referred to as Cavendish group bananas. They account for the majority of banana exports, despite only coming into existence in 1836. The cultivars Dwarf Cavendish and Grand Nain (Chiquita Banana) gained popularity in the 1950s after the previous mass-produced cultivar, Gros Michel (also an AAA group cultivar), became commercially unviable due to Panama disease, a fungus which attacks the roots of the banana plant.

Ease of transport and shelf life rather than superior taste make the Dwarf Cavendish the main export banana.

Even though it is no longer viable for large scale cultivation, Gros Michel is not extinct and is still grown in areas where Panama disease is not found. Likewise, Dwarf Cavendish and Grand Nain are in no danger of extinction, but they may leave supermarket shelves if disease makes it impossible to supply the global market. It is unclear if any existing cultivar can replace Cavendish bananas, so various hybridisation and genetic engineering programmes are attempting to create a disease-resistant, mass-market banana.

Export bananas are picked green, and ripen in special rooms upon arrival in the destination country. These rooms are air-tight and filled with ethylene gas to induce ripening. The vivid yellow colour normally associated with supermarket bananas is in fact a side effect of the artificial ripening process. Flavor and texture are also affected by ripening temperature. Bananas are refrigerated to between 13.5 and 15 °C (56 and 59 °F) during transport. At lower temperatures, ripening permanently stalls, and turns the bananas gray as cell walls break down. The skin of ripe bananas quickly blackens in the 4 °C (39 °F) environment of a domestic refrigerator, although the fruit inside remains unaffected.

Tree-ripened" Cavendish bananas have a greenish-yellow appearance which changes to a brownish-yellow as they ripen further. Although both flavor and texture of tree-ripened bananas is generally regarded as superior to any type of green-picked fruit, this reduces shelf life to only 7-10 days.

Bananas can be ordered by the retailer "ungassed", and may show up at the supermarket fully green. "Guineo Verde", or green bananas that have not been gassed will never fully ripen before becoming rotten. Instead of fresh eating, these bananas are best suited to cooking, as seen in Mexican culinary dishes.

A 2008 study reported that ripe bananas fluoresce when exposed to ultraviolet light. This property is attributed to the degradation of chlorophyll leading to the accumulation of a fluorescent product in the skin of the fruit. The chlorophyll breakdown product is stabilized by a propionate ester group. Banana-plant leaves also fluoresce in the same way. Green bananas do not fluoresce. The study suggested that this allows animals which can see light in the ultraviolet spectrum (tetrachromats and pentachromats) to more easily detect ripened bananas.

Storage and Transport

Bananas must be transported over long distances from the tropics to world markets. To obtain maximum shelf life, harvest comes before the fruit is mature. The fruit requires careful handling, rapid transport to ports, cooling, and refrigerated shipping. The goal is to prevent the bananas from producing their natural ripening agent, ethylene. This technology allows storage and transport for 3-4 weeks at 13 ℃ (55 ℉). On arrival, bananas are held at about 17 ℃ (63 ℉) and treated with a low concentration of ethylene. After a few days, the fruit begins to ripen and is distributed for final sale. Unripe bananas can not be held in home refrigerators because they suffer from the cold. Ripe bananas can be held for a few days at home. If bananas are too green, they can be put in a brown paper bag with an apple or tomato overnight to speed up the ripening process. They can be stored indefinitely frozen, then eaten like an ice pop or cooked as a banana mush.

Carbon dioxide (which bananas produce) and ethylene absorbents extend fruit life even at high temperatures. This effect can be exploited by packing banana in a polyethylene bag and including an ethylene absorbent, e.g., potassium permanganate, on an inert carrier. The bag is then sealed with a band or string. This treatment has been shown to more than double lifespans up to 3-4 weeks without the need for refrigeration.

Bananas are a staple starch for many tropical populations. Depending upon cultivar and ripeness, the flesh can vary in taste from starchy to sweet, and texture from firm to mushy. Both the skin and inner part can be eaten raw or cooked. The banana's flavor is due, amongst other chemicals, to isoamyl acetate which is one of the main constituents of banana oil.

During the ripening process, bananas produce a plant hormone called ethylene, which indirectly affects the flavor. Among other things, ethylene stimulates the formation of amylase, an enzyme that breaks down starch into sugar, influencing the taste of bananas. The greener, less ripe bananas contain higher levels of starch and, consequently, have a "starchier" taste. On the other hand, yellow bananas taste sweeter due to higher sugar concentrations. Furthermore, ethylene signals the production of pectinase, an enzyme which breaks down the pectin between the cells of the banana, causing the banana to soften as it ripens.

Bananas are eaten deep fried, baked in their skin in a split bamboo, or steamed in glutinous rice wrapped in a banana leaf. Bananas can be made into jam. Banana pancakes are popular amongst backpackers and other travelers in South Asia and Southeast Asia. This has elicited the expression *Banana Pancake Trail* for those places in Asia that cater to this group of travelers. Banana chips are a snack produced from sliced dehydrated or fried banana or plantain, which have a dark brown colour and an intense banana taste. Dried bananas are also ground to make banana flour. Extracting juice is difficult, because when a banana is compressed, it simply turns to pulp. Bananas feature prominently in Philippine cuisine, being part of traditional dishes and desserts like *maruya, turrón,* and *halo-halo*. Most of these dishes use the Saba or Cardaba banana cultivar. Pisang goreng, bananas fried with batter similar to the Filipino *maruya*, is a popular dessert in Malaysia, Singapore, and Indonesia. A similar dish is known in the United States as banana fritters.

Plantains are used in various stews and curries or cooked, baked or mashed in much the same way as potatoes.

Seeded bananas (*Musa balbisiana*), one of the forerunners of the common domesticated banana, are sold in markets in Indonesia.

Flower

Banana hearts are used as a vegetable in South Asian and Southeast Asian cuisine, either raw or steamed with dips or cooked in soups, curries and fried foods. The flavor resembles that of artichoke. As with artichokes, both the fleshy part of the bracts and the heart are edible.

Leaves

Banana leaves are large, flexible, and waterproof. They are often used as ecologically friendly disposable food containers or as "plates" in South Asia and several Southeast Asian countries. Especially in the South Indian states of Tamil Nadu, Karnataka, Andhra Pradesh and Kerala in every occasion the food must be served in a banana leaf and as a part of the food a banana is served. Steamed with dishes they impart a subtle sweet flavor. They often serve as a wrapping for grilling food. The leaves contain the juices, protect food from burning and add a subtle flavor. In Tamil Nadu (India) leaves are fully dried and used as packing material for food stuffs and also making cups to hold liquid foods. The dried leaves are called 'Vaazhai-ch- charugu' in Tamil.

Trunk

The tender core of the banana plant's trunk is also used in South Asian and Southeast Asian cuisine, and notably in the Burmese dish mohinga.

Nutrition and Research

Bananas are an excellent source of vitamin B6 and contain moderate amounts of vitamin C, manganese and potassium.

Along with other fruits and vegetables, consumption of bananas may be associated with a reduced risk of colourectal cancer and in women, breast cancer and renal cell carcinoma

Banana ingestion may affect dopamine production in people deficient in the amino acid tyrosine, a dopamine precursor present in bananas.

In India, juice is extracted from the corm and used as a home remedy for jaundice, sometimes with the addition of honey, and for kidney stones.

Other Uses

- Banana sap from the pseudostem, peelings or flesh may be sufficiently sticky for adhesive uses.
- In regions where bananas are grown, the large leaves may be used as umbrellas when the pseudostems are tied together to form a floatation device.
- Banana peel may have capability to extract heavy metal contamination from river water, similar to other purification materials.
- Banana peel has displayed antioxidant activity in vitro, especially from unripe extracts.

Banana is an energy booster, it contains tryptophan, a type of protein that the body converts into serotonin. Serotonin is a hormone that is known to make you feel happy and improve your mood, Banana is a rich source of iron, thus it is helpful in cases of anemia and Banana is good for people who have high blood pressure because it is low in salt.

CHAPTER 6

Clementines, Cherry

Clementine

Clementine's can survive eaten fresh, now peel, as they are, or additional to a salad fruit.

They can excessively be eaten in creams, ice creams, flans, cakes, cocktails, sauces etc. The relish of the *s* is commonly use to flavour cakes, sauces or fowl. As well being tasty trimmings to things like salads or cakes, clementines are worth their weight in gold around the house. From cleaning limestone countertops to keeping flies away to even maintenance stray hairs in place, there is nearly no limit to what Clementine oranges can do. On top of that, they are a extraordinary deal during the winter months that they are in season.

Those countertops identify how hard they can be to clean. In fact, many people resort to using costly cleaners that are filled with potentially harmful chemicals.

Instead of such cleansing agents, homeowners preserve use clementines! When cut in half, lightly curved in in salt and then lightly scrubbed on the marble, the clementines competently and naturally remove stain from the surface.

Clementine oranges can level be used to keep vermin away. If cat owners find that their kitties are frequently chewing on their houseplants, they can stay the cats at bay by unevenness the leaves of the plants by means of the peels of clementines.

Cherry

The cherry is the fruit of many plants of the genus *Prunus*, and is a fleshy stone fruit. The cherry fruits of commerce are usually obtained from a limited number of species, including especially cultivars of the wild cherry, *Prunus avium*.

The name 'cherry', often as the compound term 'cherry tree', may also be applied to many other members of the genus *Prunus*, or to all members of the genus as a collective term. The fruits of many of these are not cherries, and have other common names, including plum, apricot, peach, and others. The name 'cherry' is also frequently used in reference to cherry blossom.

Many cherry fruits are members of the subgenus *Cerasus*, which is distinguished by having the flowers in small corymbs of several together (not singly, nor in racemes), and by having a smooth fruit with only a weak groove or none along one side. The subgenus is native to the temperate regions of the Northern Hemisphere, with two species in America, three in Europe, and the remainder in Asia.

Other cherry fruits are members of subgenus *Padus*.

The majority of eating cherries are derived from either *Prunus avium*, the wild cherry (sometimes called the sweet cherry), or from *Prunus cerasus*, the sour cherry.

The list below contains many *Prunus* species that bear the common name cherry, but they are not necessarily members of the subgenus *Cerasus*, or bear edible fruit. For a complete list of species, see *Prunus*. Some common names listed here have historically been used for more than one species, e.g. "rock cherry" is used as an alternative common name for both *P. prostrata* and *P. mahaleb*.

- *Prunus apetala* (Siebold & Zucc.) Franch. & Sav. - clove cherry

- *Prunus avium* (L.) L. - wild cherry, sweet cherry, mazzard or gean
- *Prunus campanulata* Maxim. - Taiwan cherry, Formosan cherry or bell-flowered cherry
- *Prunus canescens* Bois. - greyleaf cherry
- *Prunus caroliniana* Aiton - Carolina laurel cherry or laurel cherry
- *Prunus cerasoides* D. Don. - wild Himalayan cherry
- *Prunus cerasus* L. - sour cherry
- *Prunus cistena* Koehne - purpleleaf sand cherry
- *Prunus cornuta* (Wall. ex Royle) Steud. - Himalayan bird cherry
- *Prunus cuthbertii* Small - Cuthbert cherry
- *Prunus cyclamina* Koehne - cyclamen cherry or Chinese flowering cherry
- *Prunus dawyckensis* Sealy - Dawyck cherry
- *Prunus dielsiana* C.K. Schneid. - tailed-leaf cherry
- *Prunus emarginata* (Douglas ex Hook.) Walp. - Oregon cherry or bitter cherry
- *Prunus eminens* Beck German: *mittlere Weichsel* (semisour cherry)
- *Prunus fruticosa* Pall. - European dwarf cherry, dwarf cherry, Mongolian cherry or steppe cherry
- *Prunus gondouinii* (Poit. & Turpin) Rehder - duke cherry
- *Prunus grayana* Maxim. - Japanese bird cherry or Gray's bird cherry
- *Prunus humilis* Bunge - Chinese plum-cherry or humble bush cherry
- *Prunus ilicifolia* (Nutt. ex Hook. & Arn.) Walp. - hollyleaf cherry, evergreen cherry, holly-leaved cherry or islay
- *Prunus incisa* Thunb. - Fuji cherry
- *Prunus jamasakura* Siebold ex Koidz. - Japanese mountain cherry or Japanese hill cherry
- *Prunus japonica* Thunb. - Korean cherry

- *Prunus laurocerasus* L. - cherry laurel
- *Prunus lyonii* (Eastw.) Sarg. - Catalina Island cherry
- *Prunus maackii* Rupr. - Manchurian cherry or Amur chokecherry
- *Prunus mahaleb* L. - Saint Lucie cherry, rock cherry, perfumed cherry or mahaleb cherry
- *Prunus maximowiczii* Rupr. - Miyama cherry or Korean cherry
- *Prunus mume* (Siebold & Zucc.) - Chinese plum or Japanese apricot
- *Prunus myrtifolia* (L.) Urb. - West Indian cherry
- *Prunus nepaulensis* (Ser.) Steud. - Nepal bird cherry
- *Prunus nipponica* Matsum. - Takane cherry, peak cherry or Japanese alpine cherry
- *Prunus occidentalis* Sw. - western cherry laurel
- *Prunus padus* L. - bird cherry or European bird cherry
- *Prunus pensylvanica* L.f. - pin cherry, fire cherry, or wild red cherry
- *Prunus pleuradenia* Griseb. - Antilles cherry
- *Prunus prostrata* Labill. - mountain cherry, rock cherry, spreading cherry or prostrate cherry
- *Prunus pseudocerasus* Lindl. - Chinese sour cherry or false cherry
- *Prunus pumila* L. - sand cherry
- *Prunus rufa* Wall ex Hook.f. - Himalayan cherry
- *Prunus salicifolia* Kunth. - capulin, Singapore cherry or tropic cherry
- *Prunus sargentii* Rehder - Sargent's cherry or Ezo Mountain cherry
- *Prunus serotina* Ehrh. - black cherry
- *Prunus serrula* Franch. - paperbark cherry, birch bark cherry or Tibetan cherry
- *Prunus serrulata* Lindl. - Japanese cherry, hill cherry, Oriental cherry or East Asian cherry

- *Prunus speciosa* (Koidz.) Ingram - Oshima cherry
- *Prunus ssiori* Schmidt- Hokkaido bird cherry
- *Prunus stipulacea* Maxim.
- *Prunus subhirtella* Miq. - Higan cherry or spring cherry
- *Prunus takesimensis* Nakai - Takeshima flowering cherry
- *Prunus tomentosa* Thunb. - Nanking cherry, Manchu cherry, downy cherry, Shanghai cherry, Ando cherry, mountain cherry, Chinese dwarf cherry, Chinese bush cherry
- *Prunus verecunda* (Koidz.) Koehne - Korean mountain cherry
- *Prunus virginiana* L. - chokecherry
- *Prunus x yedoensis* Matsum. - Yoshino cherry or Tokyo cherry

The native range of the wild cherry extends through most of Europe, western Asia and parts of northern Africa, and the fruit has been consumed through its range since prehistoric times. A cultivated cherry is recorded as having been brought to Rome by Lucius Licinius Lucullus from northeastern Anatolia, modern day Turkey, also known as the Pontus region, in 72 BC.

A form of cherry was introduced into England at Teynham, near Sittingbourne in Kent by order of Henry VIII, who had tasted them in Flanders.

The English word cherry, French *cerise* and Spanish *cereza* all come from the classical Greek through the Latin *cerasum*, thus the ancient Roman place name *Cerasus*, today a city in northern Turkey *Giresun* from which the cherry was first exported to Europe.

Cherries contain anthocyanins, the red pigment in berries. Cherry anthocyanins have been shown to reduce pain and inflammation in rats. Anthocyanins are also potent antioxidants under active research for a variety of potential health benefits. According to a study funded by the Cherry Marketing

Institute, presented at the Experimental Biology 2008 meeting in San Diego, rats that received whole tart cherry powder mixed into a high-fat diet did not gain as much weight or build up as much body fat, and their blood showed much lower levels of inflammation indicators that have been linked to heart disease and diabetes. In addition, they had significantly lower blood levels of cholesterol and triglycerides than the other rats.

Nutritional Value

Cherries (sweet, edible parts)

Nutritional value per 100 g (3.5 oz)	
Energy	263 kJ (63 kcal)
Carbohydrates	16 g
Sugars	13 g
Dietary fibre	2 g
Fat	0.2 g
Protein	1.1 g
Vitamin C	7 mg (8%)
Iron	0.4 mg (3%)

Cherry trees also provide food for the caterpillars of several Lepidoptera.

The cultivated forms are of the species wild cherry (*P. avium*) to which most cherry cultivars belong, and the sour cherry (*P. cerasus*), which is used mainly for cooking. Both species originate in Europe and western Asia; they do not cross-pollinate. Some other species, although having edible fruit, are not grown extensively for consumption, except in northern regions where the two main species will not grow.

Irrigation, spraying, labour and their propensity to damage from rain and hail make cherries relatively expensive. Nonetheless, there is high demand for the fruit. Cherry is harvested by using shaker in commercial production. Hand picking is also widely used to harvest the fruit to avoid damage.

Cherries have a very short growing season and can grow in most temperate latitudes. The peak season for cherries is in the summer.

In Australia, they are usually at their peak in late December, in southern Europe in June, in North America in June, in south British Columbia (Canada) in July to mid August, and in the UK in mid July. In many parts of North America, they are among the first tree fruits to ripen.

In Orange, NSW - A cool climate cherry region, the season begins in mid November and finishes towards the end of January. 'Kordia' is an early variety which ripens during the beginning of December, 'Lapins peak' near the end of December, and 'Sweethearts' appear slightly later.

CHAPTER 7

Date, Durian

Date

The fruit is known as a date. The fruit's English name (through Old French), as well as the Latin species name *dactylifera*, both come from the Greek word for "finger," *dáktulos*, because of the fruit's elongated shape. Dates are oval-cylindrical, 3-7 cm long, and 2-3 cm diameter, and when unripe, range from bright red to bright yellow in colour, depending on variety. Dates contain a single seed about 2-2.5 cm long and 6-8 mm thick. Three main cultivar groups of date exist: soft (e.g. 'Barhee', 'Halawy', 'Khadrawy', 'Medjool'), semi-dry (e.g. 'Dayri', 'Deglet Noor', 'Zahdi'), and dry (e.g. 'Thoory'). The type of fruit depends on the glucose, fructose and sucrose content.

The date palm is dioecious, having separate male and female plants. They can be easily grown from seed, but only 50 per cent of seedlings will be female and hence fruit bearing, and dates from seedling plants are often smaller and of poorer quality. Most commercial plantations thus use cuttings of heavily cropping cultivars. Plants grown from cuttings will fruit 2-3 years earlier than seedling plants.

Dates are naturally wind pollinated but in both traditional oasis horticulture and in the modern commercial orchards they are entirely pollinated manually. Natural pollination occurs with about an equal number of male and female plants.

However, with assistance, one male can pollinate up to 100 females. Since the males are of value only as pollinators, this allows the growers to use their resources for many more fruit producing female plants. Some growers do not even maintain any male plants as male flowers become available at local markets at pollination time. Manual pollination is done by skilled labourers on ladders. In some areas such as Iraq the pollinator climbs the tree using a special climbing tool that wraps around the tree trunk and the climber's back to keep him attached to the trunk while climbing. Less often the pollen may be blown onto the female flowers by a wind machine.

Parthenocarpic cultivars are available but the seedless fruit is smaller and of lower quality.

Dates ripen in four stages, which are known throughout the world by their Arabic names *kimri* (unripe), *khlal* (full-size, crunchy), *rutab* (ripe, soft), *tamr* (ripe, sun-dried). A 100 gram portion of fresh dates is a source of vitamin C and supplies 230 kcal (960 kJ) of energy. Since dates contain relatively little water, they do not become much more concentrated upon drying, although the vitamin C is lost in the process.

Dates are an important traditional crop in Turkey, Iraq, Arabia, and north Africa west to Morocco and are mentioned more than 50 times in the Bible. In Islamic countries, dates and yogurt or milk are a traditional first meal when the sun sets during Ramadan. Dates (especially Medjool and Deglet Noor) are also cultivated in southern California, Arizona and southern Florida in the United States.

Date palms can take 4 to 8 years after planting before they will bear fruit, and produce viable yields for commercial harvest between 7 to 10 years. Mature date palms can produce 80-120 kilograms (176-264 lb) of dates per harvest season, although they do not all ripen at the same time so several harvests are required. In order to get fruit of marketable quality, the bunches of dates must be thinned and bagged or covered before ripening so that the remaining fruits grow larger and are protected from weather and pests such as birds.

Dry or soft dates are eaten out-of-hand, or may be pitted and stuffed with fillings such as almonds, walnuts, candied orange and lemon peel, tahini, marzipan or cream cheese. Pitted dates are also referred to as *stoned dates*. Partially dried pitted dates may be glazed with glucose syrup for use as a snack food. Dates can also be chopped and used in a range of sweet and savory dishes, from tajines (tagines) in Morocco to puddings, ka'ak (types of Arab cookies) and other dessert items. Date nut bread, a type of cake, is very popular in the United States, especially around holidays. Dates are also processed into cubes, paste called "'ajwa", spread, date syrup or "honey" called "dibs" or "rub" in Libya, powder (date sugar), vinegar or alcohol. Recent innovations include chocolate-covered dates and products such as sparkling date juice, used in some Islamic countries as a non-alcoholic version of champagne, for special occasions and religious times such as Ramadan.

Dates can also be dehydrated, ground and mixed with grain to form a nutritious stockfeed. Dried dates are fed to camels, horses and dogs in the Sahara. In northern Nigeria, dates and peppers added to the native beer are believed to make it less intoxicating.

Young date leaves are cooked and eaten as a vegetable, as is the terminal bud or heart, though its removal kills the palm. The finely ground seeds are mixed with flour to make bread in times of scarcity. The flowers of the date palm are also edible. Traditionally the female flowers are the most available for sale and weigh 300-400 grams. The flower buds are used in salad or ground with dried fish to make a condiment for bread.

Dates provide a wide range of essential nutrients, and are a very good source of dietary potassium. The sugar content of ripe dates is about 80 per cent; the remainder consists of protein, fibre, and trace elements including boron, cobalt, copper, fluorine, magnesium, manganese, selenium, and zinc. The glycemic index for three different varieties of dates are 35.5 (*khalas*), 49.7 (*barhi*) and 30.5 (*bo ma'an*).

In India and Pakistan, North Africa, Ghana, and Côte d'Ivoire, date palms are tapped for the sweet sap, which is converted into palm sugar (known as *jaggery* or *gur*), molasses or alcoholic beverages. In North Africa the sap obtained from tapping palm trees is known as lagbi. If left for a sufficient period of time (typically hours, depending on the temperature) lagbi easily becomes an alcoholic drink. Special skill is required when tapping the palm tree so that it does not die.

In Southeast Spain (where a large date plantation exists including UNESCO protected Palmeral of Elche) dates (usually pitted with fried almond) are served wrapped in bacon and shallow fried.It is also used to make Jallab.

Date seeds are soaked and ground up for animal feed. Their oil is suitable for use in soap and cosmetics. They can also be processed chemically as a source of oxalic acid. The seeds are also burned to make charcoal for silversmiths, and can be strung in necklaces. Date seeds are also ground and used in the manner of coffee beans, or as an additive to coffee.

Stripped fruit clusters are used as brooms. In Pakistan, a viscous, thick syrup made from the ripe fruits is used as a coating for leather bags and pipes to prevent leaking.

Date palm sap is used to make palm syrup and numerous edible products derived from the syrup.

Date palm leaves are used for Palm Sunday in the Christian religion. In North Africa, they are commonly used for making huts. Mature leaves are also made into mats, screens, baskets and fans. Processed leaves can be used for insulating board. Dried leaf petioles are a source of cellulose pulp, used for walking sticks, brooms, fishing floats and fuel. Leaf sheaths are prized for their scent, and fibre from them is also used for rope, coarse cloth, and large hats. The leaves are also used as a lulav in the Jewish holiday of Sukkot.

Date palm wood is used for posts and rafters for huts; it is lighter than coconut and not very durable. It is also used for construction such as bridges and aqueducts, and parts of dhows. Leftover wood is burnt for fuel.

Where craft traditions still thrive, such as in Oman, the palm tree is the most versatile of all indigenous plants, and virtually every part of the tree is utilized to make functional items ranging from rope and baskets to beehives, fishing boats, and traditional dwellings.

Dates have a high tannin content and are used medicinally as a detersive (having cleansing power) and astringent in intestinal troubles. As an infusion, decoction, syrup, or paste, dates may be administered for sore throat, colds, bronchial catarrh, and taken to relieve fever and a number of other complaints. One traditional belief is that it can counteract alcohol intoxication. The seed powder is also used in some traditional medicines. Because of their laxative quality, dates are considered to be good at preventing constipation.

A gum that exudes from the wounded trunk is employed in India for treating diarrhea and genito-urinary ailments. The roots are used against toothache. The pollen yields an estrogenic principle, estrone, and has a gonadotropic effect on young rats.

Durian

The durian is the fruit of several tree species belonging to the genus *Durio* and the Malvaceae family (although some taxonomists place *Durio* in a distinct family, Durionaceae). Widely known and revered in southeast Asia as the "king of fruits", the durian is distinctive for its large size, unique odour, and formidable thorn-covered husk. The fruit can grow as large as 30 centimetres (12 in) long and 15 centimetres (6 in) in diameter, and it typically weighs one to three kilograms (2 to 7 lb). Its shape ranges from oblong to round, the colour of its husk green to brown, and its flesh pale yellow to red, depending on the species.

The edible flesh emits a distinctive odour, strong and penetrating even when the husk is intact. Some people regard the durian as fragrant; others find the aroma overpowering and offensive. The smell evokes reactions from deep appreciation to intense disgust, and has been described variously as almonds, rotten onions, turpentine and gym socks. The odour has led to the fruit's banishment from certain hotels and public transportation in southeast Asia.

The durian, native to Brunei, Indonesia and Malaysia, has been known to the Western world for about 600 years. The 19th-century British naturalist Alfred Russel Wallace famously described its flesh as "a rich custard highly flavoured with almonds". The flesh can be consumed at various stages of ripeness, and it is used to flavour a wide variety of savoury and sweet edibles in Southeast Asian cuisines. The seeds can also be eaten when cooked.

There are 30 recognised *Durio* species, at least nine of which produce edible fruit. *Durio zibethinus* is the only species available in the international market: other species are sold in their local regions. There are hundreds of durian cultivars; many consumers express preferences for specific cultivars, which fetch higher prices in the market.

The unusual flavour and odour of the fruit have prompted many people to express diverse and passionate views ranging from deep appreciation to intense disgust. Writing in 1856, the British naturalist Alfred Russel Wallace provides a much-quoted description of the flavour of the durian.

The five cells are silky-white within, and are filled with a mass of firm, cream-coloured pulp, containing about three seeds each. This pulp is the edible part, and its consistence and flavour are indescribable. A rich custard highly flavoured with almonds gives the best general idea of it, but there are occasional wafts of flavour that call to mind cream-cheese, onion-sauce, sherry-wine, and other incongruous dishes. Then there is a rich glutinous smoothness in the pulp which nothing else possesses, but which adds to its delicacy. It is neither acid nor sweet nor juicy; yet it wants neither of these qualities, for it is in itself perfect. It produces no nausea or other bad effect, and the more you eat of it the less you feel inclined to stop. In fact, to eat Durians is a new sensation worth a voyage to the East to experience as producing a food of the most exquisite flavour it is unsurpassed.

Researcher described himself as being at first reluctant to try it because of the aroma, "but in Borneo I found a ripe fruit on the ground, and, eating it out of doors, I at once became a confirmed Durian eater". He cited one traveller from "it is of such an excellent taste that it surpasses in flavour all other fruits of the world, according to those who have tasted it". He cites another writer: "To those not used to it, it seems at first to smell like rotten onions, but immediately after they have tasted it they prefer it to all other food. The natives give it honourable titles, exalt it, and make verses on it".

While researcher cautions that "the smell of the ripe fruit is certainly at first disagreeable", later descriptions by westerners are more graphic. British novelist Anthony Burgess writes that eating durian is "like eating sweet raspberry blancmange in the lavatory."

Other comparisons have been made with the civet, sewage, stale vomit, skunk spray and used surgical swabs. The wide range of descriptions for the odour of durian may have a great deal to do with the variability of durian odour itself. Durians from different species or clones can have significantly different aromas; for example, red durian (*D. dulcis*) has a deep caramel flavour with a turpentine odour while red-fleshed durian (*D. graveolens*) emits a fragrance of roasted almonds. Among the varieties of *D. zibethinus*, Thai varieties are sweeter in flavour and less odourous than Malay ones. The degree of ripeness has an effect on the flavour as well. Three scientific analyses of the composition of durian aroma — from 1972, 1980, and 1995 — each found a mix of volatile compounds including esters, ketones, and different sulphur compounds, with no agreement on which may be primarily responsible for the distinctive odour.

This strong odour can be detected half a mile away by animals, thus luring them. In addition, the fruit is extremely appetising to a variety of animals, including squirrels, mouse deer, pigs, orangutan, elephants, and even carnivorous tigers. While some of these animals eat the fruit and dispose of the seed under the parent plant, others swallow the seed with the fruit and then transport it some distance before excreting, with the seed being dispersed as a result. The thorny, armoured covering of the fruit discourages smaller animals; larger animals are more likely to transport the seeds far from the parent tree.

According to Larousse Gastronomique, the durian fruit is ready to eat when its husk begins to crack. However, the ideal stage of ripeness to be enjoyed varies from region to region in Southeast Asia and by species. Some species grow so tall that they can only be collected once they have fallen to the ground, whereas most cultivars of *D. zibethinus* are nearly always cut from the tree and allowed to ripen while waiting to be sold. Some people in southern Thailand prefer their durians relatively young when the clusters of fruit within the shell are still crisp in texture and mild in flavour. For some people in northern Thailand, the preference is for the fruit to be soft and aromatic. In Malaysia and Singapore, most consumers prefer the fruit to be as ripe and pungent in aroma as possible and may even risk allowing the fruit to continue ripening after its husk has already cracked open. In this state, the flesh becomes richly creamy, slightly alcoholic, the aroma pronounced and the flavour highly complex.

The various preferences regarding ripeness among consumers make it hard to issue general statements about choosing a "good" durian. A durian that falls off the tree continues to ripen for two to four days, but after five or six days most would consider it overripe and unpalatable. The usual advice for a durian consumer choosing a whole fruit in the market is to examine the quality of the stem or stalk which loses moisture as it ages: a big, solid stem is a sign of freshness. Reportedly, unscrupulous merchants wrap, paint, or remove the stalks altogether. Another frequent piece of advice is to shake the fruit and listen for the sound of the seeds moving within, indicating the durian is very ripe and the pulp has dried out a bit.

The durian has been known and consumed in southeastern Asia since prehistoric times, but has only been known to the western world for about 600 years. The earliest known European reference to the durian is the record of Niccolò Da Conti, who travelled to southeastern Asia in the 15th century. The Portuguese physician Garcia de Orta described durians in *Colóquios dos simples e drogas da India* published in 1563. In 1741, *Herbarium Amboinense* by the German botanist Georg Eberhard Rumphius was published, providing the most detailed and accurate account of durians for over a century. The genus *Durio* has a complex taxonomy that has seen the subtraction and addition of many species since it was created by Rumphius. During the early stages of its taxonomical study, there was some confusion between durian and the soursop (*Annona muricata*), for both of these species had thorny green fruit. It is also interesting to note the Malay name for the soursop is *durian Belanda,* meaning *Dutch durian*. In the 18th century, Johann Anton Weinmann considered the durian to belong to Castaneae as its fruit was similar to the horse chestnut.

D. zibethinus was introduced into Ceylon by the Portuguese in the 16th century and was reintroduced many times later. It has been planted in the Americas but confined to botanical gardens. The first seedlings were sent from the Royal Botanic Gardens, Kew, to Auguste Saint-Arroman of Dominica in 1884.

In southeastern Asia the durian has been cultivated for centuries at the village level, probably since the late 18th century, and commercially since the mid-20th century. In *My Tropic Isle*, Australian author and naturalist Edmund James Banfield tells how, in the early 20th century, a friend in Singapore sent him a durian seed, which he planted and cared for on his tropical island off the north coast of Queensland.

Since the early 1990s, the domestic and international demand for durian in the Association of Southeast Asian Nations (ASEAN) region has increased significantly, partly due to the increasing affluence of Asia.

Durian fruit is used to flavour a wide variety of sweet edibles such as traditional Malay candy, ice kacang, dodol, lempuk , rose biscuits, and, with a touch of modern innovation, ice cream, milkshakes, mooncakes, Yule logs and cappuccino. *Es durian* (durian ice cream) is a popular dessert in Indonesia, sold at street side stall in Indonesian cities, especially in Java. Pulut Durian is glutinous rice steamed with coconut milk and served with ripened durian. In Sabah, red durian is fried with onions and chilli and served as a side dish. Red-fleshed durian is traditionally added to *sayur*, an Indonesian soup made from freshwater fish. *Ikan brengkes* is fish cooked in a durian-based sauce, traditional in Sumatra. *Tempoyak* refers to fermented durian, usually made from lower quality durian that is unsuitable for direct consumption. Tempoyak can be eaten either cooked or uncooked, is normally eaten with rice, and can also be used for making curry. Sambal Tempoyak is a Sumatran dish made from the fermented durian fruit, coconut milk, and a collection of spicy ingredients known as sambal.

In Thailand, durian is often eaten fresh with sweet sticky rice, and blocks of durian paste are sold in the markets, though much of the paste is adulterated with pumpkin. Unripe durians may be cooked as a vegetable, except in the Philippines, where all uses are sweet rather than savoury. Malaysians make both sugared and salted preserves from durian. When durian is minced with salt, onions and vinegar, it is called *boder*. The durian seeds, which are the size of chestnuts, can be eaten whether they are boiled, roasted or fried in coconut oil, with a texture that is similar to taro or yam, but stickier. In Java, the seeds are sliced thin and cooked with sugar as a confection. Uncooked durian seeds are toxic due to cyclopropene fatty acids and should not be ingested. Young leaves and shoots of the durian are occasionally cooked as greens. Sometimes the ash of the burned rind is added to special cakes. The petals of durian flowers are eaten in the North Sumatra province of Indonesia, while in the Moluccas islands the husk of the durian fruit is used as fuel to smoke fish. The nectar and pollen of the durian flower that honeybees collect is an important honey source, but the characteristics of the honey are unknown.

Nutritional Value per 100 g (3.5 oz)

Energy	615 kJ (147 kcal)
Carbohydrates	27.09 g
Dietary fibre	3.8 g
Fat	5.33 g
Protein	1.47 g
Water	65g
Vitamin C	19.7 mg (24%)
Potassium	436 mg (9%)

Durian fruit contains a high amount of sugar, vitamin C, potassium, and the serotonergic amino acid tryptophan, and is a good source of carbohydrates, proteins, and fats. It is recommended as a good source of raw fats by several raw food advocates, while others classify it as a high-glycemic food, recommending to minimise its consumption.

In Malaysia, a decoction of the leaves and roots used to be prescribed as an antipyretic. The leaf juice is applied on the head of a fever patient. The most complete description of the medicinal use of the durian as remedies for fevers is a Malay prescription, collected by Burkill and Haniff in 1930. It instructs the reader to boil the roots of *Hibiscus rosa-sinensis* with the roots of *Durio zibethinus*, *Nephelium longan*, *Nephelium mutabile* and *Artocarpus integrifolia*, and drink the decoction or use it as a poultice.

Southeast Asian traditional beliefs, as well as traditional Chinese medicine, consider the durian fruit to have warming properties liable to cause excessive sweating. The traditional method to counteract this is to pour water into the empty shell of the fruit after the pulp has been consumed and drink it. An alternative method is to eat the durian in accompaniment with mangosteen, which is considered to have cooling properties. Pregnant women or people with high blood pressure are traditionally advised not to consume durian.

Another common local belief is that the durian is harmful when eaten with coffee or alcoholic beverages. The latter belief can be traced back at least to the 18th century when Rumphius stated that one should not drink alcohol after eating durians as it will cause indigestion and bad breath. In 1929, J.D. Gimlette wrote in his *Malay Poisons and Charm Cures* that the durian fruit must not be eaten with brandy. In 1981, J.R. Croft wrote in his *Bombacaceae: In Handbooks of the Flora of Papua New Guinea* that "a feeling of morbidity" often follows the consumption of alcohol too soon after eating durian. Several medical investigations on the validity of this belief have been conducted with varying conclusions, though a study by the University of Tsukuba finds the fruit's high sulphur content caused the body to inhibit the activity of aldehyde dehydrogenase, causing a 70 per cent reduction of the ability to clear toxins from the body.

The Javanese believe durian to have aphrodisiac qualities, and impose a set of rules on what may or may not be consumed with it or shortly thereafter. A saying in Indonesian, *durian jatuh sarung naik,* meaning "the durians fall and the sarongs come up", refers to this belief. The warnings against the supposed lecherous quality of this fruit soon spread to the West—the Swedenborgian philosopher Herman Vetterling commented on so-called "erotic properties" of the durian in the early 20th century.

A durian falling on a person's head can cause serious injuries because it is heavy, armed with sharp thorns, and can fall from a significant height. Wearing a hardhat is recommended when collecting the fruit. Alfred Russel Wallace writes that death rarely ensues from it, because the copious effusion of blood prevents the inflammation which might otherwise take place. A common saying is that a durian has eyes and can see where it is falling because the fruit allegedly never falls during daylight hours when people may be hurt. A saying in Indonesian, *ketiban durian runtuh,* which translates to "getting a fallen durian", means receiving an unexpected luck or fortune. Nevertheless, signs warning people not to linger under durian trees are found in Indonesia.

A naturally spineless variety of durian growing wild in Davao, Philippines, was discovered in the 1960s; fruits borne from these seeds also lacked spines. Since the bases of the scales develop into spines as the fruit matures, sometimes spineless durians are produced artificially by scraping scales off immature fruits.

CHAPTER 8

Figs

Fig fruits are in bell-shaped, with a wide, flat bottom narrowing top. When the fruit ripens, the top will bend, forming like a "neck".Figs can be of varities of colours such as brown, purple, green, yellow or black, and vary in size. The skin is slightly wrinkled and leathery.They are often will be in the dried stage for preservation since the fresh fruits are highly perishable. The fig flowers develop inside the fruit and cannot be visible. Fig is naturally rich in health benefiting phyto-nutrients, anti-oxidants vitamins and minerals.Dried figs contains concentrated source of minerals and vitamins.

The Common Fig is widely known for its edible fruit throughout the Mediterranean and Middle Eastern region, Iran, Turkey, Pakistan, northern India, and also in other areas of the world with a similar climate, including Arkansas, Louisiana, California, Georgia, Oregon, Texas, South Carolina, and Washington in the United States, south-western British Columbia in Canada, Durango, Nuevo León and Coahuila in northeastern Mexico, as well as areas of Argentina, Australia, Chile, Peru, and South Africa.

Two crops of figs are potentially produced each year. The first or breva crop develops in the spring on last year's shoot growth: In contrast, the main fig crop develops on the current year's shoot growth and ripens in the late summer or fall. The main crop is generally superior in both quantity and quality than the breva crop. However, some cultivars produce good breva crops (e.g., Black Mission, Croisic, and Ventura).

There are basically three varieties of common figs:

1. Caducous (or Smyrna) figs require pollination by the fig wasp and caprifigs to develop crops. Some cultivars are Calimyrna, Marabout, and Zidi.
2. Persistent (or Common) figs do not need pollination; fruit develop through parthenocarpic means. This is the variety of fig most commonly grown by home gardeners. Adriatic, Black Mission, Brown Turkey, Brunswick, and Celeste are some representative cultivars.
3. Intermediate (or San Pedro) figs do not need pollination to set the breva crop, but do need pollination, at least in some regions, for the main crop. Examples are Lampeira, King, and San Pedro.

Figs plants are easy to propagate through several methods. Propagation using seeds is not the preferred method since vegetative methods exist that are quicker and more reliable, that is, they do not yield the inedible caprifigs. However, those desiring to can plant seeds of dried figs with moist sphagnum moss or other media in a zip lock bag and expect germination in a few weeks to several months. The tiny plants can be transplanted out little by little once the leaves open, and despite the tiny initial size can grow to 1 foot (30 cm) or more one year from planting seeds.

For propagation in the mid-summer months, air layer new growth in August (mid-summer) or insert hardened off 15-25 cm (6-10 inches) shoots into moist perlite or a sandy soil mix, keeping the cuttings shaded until new growth begins; then gradually move them into full sun. An alternative propagation method is bending over a taller branch, scratching the bark to reveal the green inner bark, then pinning the scratched area tightly to the ground. Within a few weeks, roots will develop and the branch can be clipped from the mother plant and transplanted where desired.

For spring propagation, before the tree starts growth, cut 15-25 cm (6-10 inches) shoots that have healthy buds at their ends, and set into a moist perlite and/or sandy soil mix located in the shade. Once the cuttings start to produce leaves, bury them up to the bottom leaf to give the plant a good start in the desired location.

Figs can also be found in continental climate with hot summer, as far north as Hungary and Moravia, and can be harvested up to four times per year. Thousands of cultivars, most named, have been developed or come into existence as human migration brought the fig to many places outside its natural range. It has been an important food crop for thousands of years, and was also thought to be highly beneficial in the diet.

The edible fig is one of the first plants that was cultivated by humans. Nine subfossil figs of a parthenocarpic type dating to about 9400-9200 BC were found in the early Neolithic village Gilgal I (in the Jordan Valley, 13 km north of Jericho). The find predates the domestication of wheat, barley, and legumes, and may thus be the first known instance of agriculture. It is proposed that they may have been planted and cultivated intentionally, one thousand years before the next crops were domesticated (wheat and rye).

Figs were also a common food source for the Romans. Cato the Elder, in his *De Agri Cultura*, lists several strains of figs grown at the time he wrote his handbook: the Mariscan, African, Herculanean, Saguntine, and the black Tellanian . The fruits were used, among other things, to fatten geese for the production of a precursor of foie gras.

Figs can be eaten fresh or dried, and used in jam-making. Most commercial production is in dried or otherwise processed forms, since the ripe fruit does not transport well, and once picked does not keep well.

Figs are one of the highest plant sources of calcium and fibre. According to USDA data for the Mission variety, dried figs are richest in fibre, copper, manganese, magnesium, potassium, calcium, and vitamin K, relative to human needs. They have smaller amounts of many other nutrients. Figs have a laxative effect and contain many antioxidants. They are good source of flavonoids and polyphenols including gallic acid, chlorogenic acid, syringic acid, (+)-catechin, (-)-epicatechin and rutin. In one study, a 40-gram portion of dried figs (two medium size figs) produced a significant increase in plasma antioxidant capacity

Dried or fresh Figs act as a natural laxative. It is high in dietary fibre and promotes healthy bowel movement function.Every three grams of this fruit is loaded with every five grams of fibre. Consumption of figs is very good in preventing constipation.

Weight Loss

Figs are rich in dietary fibre.Fibre and fibre related foods have positive effect on weight management. Women who increased their fibre intake with supplements significantly decreased their energy intake, yet their hunger and satiety scores did not change. Fig is an excellent source of dietary fibre. It is an efficient food to lose weight.

Lower Cholesterol

Figs are good sources of fibre. It contain soluble fibre called pectin that undergoes through the digestive system, mops up waste cholesterol and push them out from the body. So, a regular diet of figs can help you to cut down your cholesterol in all regular ways.

Coronary Heart Disease

Figs are rich in phenol and omega-6 fatty acids. These are natural heart boosters,so that it might able to reduce the risk of coronary heart diseases

Colon Cancer

It is also believed that the fibre in figs cancer mop up and usher out causing substances,thus reducing the risk of various types of cancer. Figs are especially good in preventing colon cancer.

Menopausal Breast Cancer

Fibre content in figs provides protection against breast cancer. 51,823 menopausal women for an average of 8.3 years showed a 34 per cent reduction in breast cancer risk for those consuming the most fibre fruit compared to those consuming the least. In addition, women who had ever used hormone replacement, those consuming the most fibre, especially cereal fibre, had a 50 per cent reduction in their risk of breast cancer compared to those consuming the least.Fruits richest in fibre include apples, dates, figs, pears and prunes.

Diabetes

People suffering from diabetes should adopt high fibre diet. The leaves of the fig tree are one of the edible parts that are rich in fibre. The leaves of fig contain antidiabetic properties that can reduce the amount of insulin needed by the persons suffering from diabetes to those who have to take insulin injections. Liquid extract made from fig leaves was added to the breakfast in order to reduce diabetes and lowering of insulin injections.

Hypertension

People used to take more sodium in the form of salt. Low potassium or low intake of potassium rich foods and high sodium level may lead to hypertension. Figs are high in potassium but low in sodium. So, it helps to avoid hypertension.

Sexual Weakness

Figs are known for reducing sexual weakness. Soak 2-3 figs in milk overnight and eat them in the morning to enhance your sexual power. It also helps in gaining weight hence by consuming figs sexual power can be increased.

Piles

Figs are efficient for your digestive system.It provides good in digestion and improves body metabolism. Daily intake of figs is very beneficial to those who are suffering from piles or hemorrhoids.

CHAPTER 9

Grape, Grape Fruit, Guava Fruit

Grape

A grape is a non-climacteric fruit, specifically a berry, and from the deciduous woody vines of the genus *Vitis*. Grapes can be eaten raw or they can be used for making jam, juice, jelly, wine, grape seed extracts, raisins, vinegar, and grape seed oil.

Grapes are a type of fruit that grow in clusters of 15 to 300, and can be crimson, black, dark blue, yellow, green, orange, and pink. "White" grapes are actually green in colour, and are evolutionarily derived from the purple grape. Mutations in two regulatory genes of white grapes turn off production of anthocyanins which are responsible for the colour of purple grapes. Anthocyanins and other pigment chemicals of the larger family of polyphenols in purple grapes are responsible for the varying shades of purple in red wines. Grapes are also used in some kinds of confectionery. Grapes are typically an ellipsoid shape resembling a prolate spheroid.

Most grapes come from cultivars of *Vitis vinifera*, the European grapevine native to the Mediterranean and Central Asia. Minor amounts of fruit and wine come from American and Asian species such as:

- *Vitis labrusca*, the North American table and grape juice grapevines (including the concord cultivar), sometimes used for wine, are native to the Eastern United States and Canada.

- *Vitis riparia*, a wild vine of North America, is sometimes used for winemaking and for jam. It is native to the entire Eastern U.S. and north to Quebec.
- *Vitis rotundifolia*, the muscadines, used for jams and wine, are native to the Southeastern United States from Delaware to the Gulf of Mexico.
- *Vitis amurensis* is the most important Asian species.

Grape juice is obtained from crushing and blending grapes into a liquid. The juice is often sold in stores or fermented and made into wine, brandy, or vinegar. In the wine industry, grape juice that contains 7-23 per cent of pulp, skins, stems and seeds is often referred to as "must". In North America, the most common grape juice is purple and made from Concord grapes while white grape juice is commonly made from Niagara grapes, both of which are varieties of native American grapes, a different species from European wine grapes. In California, Sultana (known there as Thompson Seedless) grapes are sometimes diverted from the raisin or table market to produce white juice.

Commercially cultivated grapes can usually be classified as either table or wine grapes, based on their intended method of consumption: eaten raw (table grapes) or used to make wine (wine grapes). While almost all of them belong to the same species, *Vitis vinifera*, table and wine grapes have significant differences, brought about through selective breeding. Table grape cultivars tend to have large, seedless fruit (see below) with relatively thin skin. Wine grapes are smaller, usually seeded, and have relatively thick skins (a desirable characteristic in winemaking, since much of the aroma in wine comes from the skin). Wine grapes also tend to be very sweet: they are harvested at the time when their juice is approximately 24 per cent sugar by weight. By comparison, commercially produced "100 per cent grape juice", made from table grapes is usually around 15 per cent sugar by weight.

Although grape seeds contain many nutrients, some consumers choose seedless grapes; seedless cultivars now make up the overwhelming majority of table grape plantings. Because grapevines are vegetatively propagated by cuttings, the lack of seeds does not present a problem for reproduction. It is an issue for breeders, who must either use a seeded variety as the female parent or rescue embryos early in development using tissue culture techniques.

There are several sources of the seedlessness trait, and essentially all commercial cultivators get it from one of three sources: Thompson Seedless, Russian Seedless, and Black Monukka, all being cultivars of *Vitis vinifera*. There are currently more than a dozen varieties of seedless grapes. Several, such as Einset Seedless, Benjamin Gunnels's Prime seedless grapes, Reliance and Venus, have been specifically cultivated for hardiness and quality in the relatively cold climates of northeastern United States and southern Ontario.

An offset to the improved eating quality of seedlessness is the loss of potential health benefits provided by the enriched phytochemical content of grape seeds.

Anthocyanins tend to be the main polyphenolics in purple grapes whereas flavan-3-ols (i.e. catechins) are the more abundant phenolic in white varieties. Total phenolic content, a laboratory index of antioxidant strength, is higher in purple varieties due almost entirely to anthocyanin density in purple grape skin compared to absence of anthocyanins in white grape skin. It is these anthocyanins that are attracting the efforts of scientists to define their properties for human health. Phenolic content of grape skin varies with cultivar, soil composition, climate, geographic origin, and cultivation practices or exposure to diseases, such as fungal infections.

Red wine may offer health benefits more so than white because potentially beneficial compounds are present in grape skin, and only red wine is fermented with skins. The amount of fermentation time a wine spends in contact with grape skins is an important determinant of its resveratrol content.

Ordinary non-muscadine red wine contains between 0.2 and 5.8 mg/L, depending on the grape variety, because it is fermented with the skins, allowing the wine to absorb the resveratrol. By contrast, a white wine contains lower phenolic contents because it is fermented after removal of skins.

Wines produced from muscadine grapes may contain more than 40 mg/L, an exceptional phenolic content. In muscadine skins, ellagic acid, myricetin, quercetin, kaempferol, and trans-resveratrol are major phenolics. Contrary to previous results, ellagic acid and not resveratrol is the major phenolic in muscadine grapes.

The flavonols syringetin, syringetin 3-O-galactoside, laricitrin and laricitrin 3-O-galactoside are also found in purple grape but absent in white grape.

Seed Constituents

Since the 1980s, biochemical and medical studies have demonstrated significant antioxidant properties of grape seed oligomeric proanthocyanidins. Together with tannins, polyphenols and polyunsaturated fatty acids, these seed constituents display inhibitory activities against several experimental disease models, including cancer, heart failure and other disorders of oxidative stress.

Grape seed oil from crushed seeds is used in cosmeceuticals and skincare products for many perceived health benefits. Grape seed oil is notable for its high contents of tocopherols (vitamin E), phytosterols, and polyunsaturated fatty acids such as linoleic acid, oleic acid and alpha-linolenic acid.

Commercial juice products from Concord grapes have been applied in medical research studies, showing potential benefits against the onset stage of cancer, platelet aggregation and other risk factors of atherosclerosis, loss of physical performance and mental acuity during aging and hypertension in humans.

The health benefits of grapes include its ablity to treat constipation, indigestion, fatigue, kidney disorders, macular degeneration and prevention of cataract. Grapes, one of the most delicious fruits, are rich sources of vitamins A, C, B_6 and folate in addition to essential minerals like potassium, calcium, iron, phosphorus, magnesium and selenium. Grapes contain flavonoids that are very powerful antioxidants, which can reduce the damage caused by free radicals and slacken ageing.

Grapes, owing to their high nutrient content, play an important role in ensuring a healthy and robust life.

- **Benefits:** Some of the health benefits of grapes include the following:
  - *Asthma:* Due to its eminent therapeutic value, grapes can be used for cure of asthma. In addition to it, the assimilatory power of grapes is also higher. It increases the moisture present in lungs.
  - *Heart diseases:* Grapes increase the nitric oxide levels in the blood, which prevents blood clots thereby reducing the chances of heart attacks. In addition the antioxidant present in grapes prevents the oxidation of LDL cholesterol, which blocks the blood vessels.
  - *Migraine:* Ripe grape juice is an important home remedy for curing migraine. It should be taken early in the morning, without mixing additional water.
  - *Constipation:* Grapes are very effective in overcoming constipation. They are considered as a laxative food, as they contain organic acid, sugar and cellulose. They also relieve chronic constipation by toning up intestine and stomach.
  - *Indigestion:* Grapes play an important role in dyspepsia. They relieve heat and cure indigestion and irritation of the stomach. They are also preferred as they constitute a light food.
  - *Fatigue:* Light and white grape juice replenishes the iron content present in the body and prevents

fatigue. Though, the dark grape juice might not give an iron boost and on the other hand, decrease the iron levels. Drinking grape juice also provides you with instant energy. The anti-oxidants present in grapes also provide the needed boost to your immune system.

– *Kidney disorders:* Grapes can substantially reduce the acidity of the uric acid and helps in the elimination of the acid from the system, thereby reducing the work pressure of kidneys.

– *Breast cancer:* Through a latest study, it has been discovered that purple coloured Concord grape juice helps in preventing breast cancer. Significant reduction in mammary tumor mass of laboratory rats was seen after they were fed the grape juice on the experimental basis.

– *Alzheimer's disease:* Resveratrol, a beneficial polyphenol present in grapes reduces the levels of amyloidal-beta peptides in patients with Alzheimer's disease. Studies suggest that grapes can enhance brain health and stall the onset of neurodegenerative diseases.

– *Macular degeneration:* Grapes can prevent the age related loss of vision or macular degeneration. Three servings of grapes a day can reduce the risks of macular degeneration by over 36 per cent.

– *Prevents cataract:* Flavonoids present in grapes have antioxidants, which can reduce and fight the damage caused by free radicals such as cataract apart from cardiovascular diseases, cancer, and age related problems.

– *Blood cholesterol:* Grapes contain a compound called pterostilbene, which has the capacity to bring down cholesterol level. Saponins present in grape skin can also prevent the absorption of cholesterol by binding with it.

- *Antibacterial activity:* Red grapes have strong antibacterial and antiviral properties and can protect you from infections. They have a strong antiviral property against poliovirus and herpes simplex virus.
- *Anticancer properties:* Grapes are found to have strong anti cancer properties due to the anti-inflammatory effect of resveratrol present in grapes. It is particularly effective in colorectal cancer and breast cancer. Anthocyanins and proanthocyanidins present in grapes have properties of an anti-proliferate and can inhibit the growth of cancer causing agents. Grape juice not just prevents the risk of cancer but also suppresses the growth and propagation of cancer cells. The pigments contained in grapes enhance the overall immunity of the body.

Thus, grapes play a pivotal role in preventing innumerable health disorders and can be used as home based remedies for several ailments. Dried grapes, known as raisins, are extremely nutritious and help in many disorders including constipation, acidosis, anemia, fever, sexual weakness and help in gaining weight and eye care.

Grapefruit

The grapefruit (*Citrus* × *paradisi*) is a subtropical citrus tree known for its sour fruit, an 18th-century hybrid first bred in Barbados. When found, it was named the "forbidden fruit"; and it has also been misidentified with the pomelo or shaddock (C. *maxima*), one of the parents of this hybrid, the other being sweet orange (C. × *sinensis*).

These evergreen trees usually grow to around 5-6 meters (16-20 ft) tall, although they can reach 13-15 meters (43-49 ft). The leaves are dark green, long (up to 150 mm, 6 inches) and thin. It produces 5 cm (2 in) white four-petaled flowers. The fruit is yellow-orange skinned and largely an oblate spheroid; it ranges in diametre from 10-15 cm. The flesh is segmented and acidic, varying in colour depending on the cultivars, which include white, pink and red pulps of varying sweetness. The 1929 US Ruby Red (of the Redblush variety) has the first grapefruit patent.

The fruit has become popular since the late 19th century; before that it was only grown as an ornamental plant. The United States quickly became a major producer of the fruit, with groves in Florida, Texas, Arizona, and California. In Spanish, the fruit is known as *toronja* or *pomelo.*

One ancestor of the grapefruit was the Jamaican sweet orange (*Citrus sinensis*), itself an ancient hybrid of Asian origin; the other was the Indonesian pomelo (C. *maxima*). One story of the fruit's origins is that a certain "Captain Shaddock" brought pomelo seeds to Jamaica and bred the first fruit. However, it probably originated as a naturally-occurring hybrid.

The hybrid fruit was documented in 1750 by a Welshman, Rev. Griffith Hughes, who described specimens from Barbados. Currently, the grapefruit is said to be one of the "Seven Wonders of Barbados." It was brought to Florida by Count Odette Philippe in 1823 in what is now known as Safety Harbor. Further crosses have produced the tangelo (1905), the Minneola tangelo (1931), and the oroblanco (1984).

The grapefruit was known as the *shaddock* or *shattuck* until the 19th century. Its current name alludes to clusters of the fruit on the tree, which often appear similar to grapes. Botanically, it was not distinguished from the pomelo until the 1830s, when it was given the name *Citrus paradisi.* Its true origins were not determined until the 1940s. This led to the official name being altered to *Citrus × paradisi,* the "×" identifying its hybrid

Grapefruit can have a number of interactions with drugs, often increasing the effective potency of compounds. Grapefruit contains a number of polyphenolic compounds, including the flavanone naringin, alongside the two furanocoumarins bergamottin and dihydroxybergamottin. These inhibit the drug-metabolizing enzyme isoform CYP3A4 predominately in the small intestine, but at higher doses also inhibit hepatic CYP3A4. It is via inhibition of this enzyme that grapefruit increases the effects of a variety of drugs by increasing their bioavailability. In particular grapefruit and bitter oranges are known to interact with statins. Because of this unique property, grapefruit has a very bitter taste when mixed with milk or similar dairy products.

Grapefruit juice may be the first drug-interacting fruit juice documented, but apple and orange juices have been also implicated in interfering with etoposide, a chemotherapy drug, some beta blocker drugs used to treat high blood pressure, and cyclosporine, taken by transplant patients to prevent rejection of their new organs. Some citrus-based carbonated beverages (*e.g.*, "Sun Drop") also contain enough grapefruit juice to cause drug interactions, particularly in patients taking cyclosporine.

Unlike other fruits, grapefruit contains a large amount of naringin, and it can take up to 72 hours before the effects of the naringin on the CYP3A4 enzyme are seen. This is particularly problematic due to the fact that only 4 oz of grapefruit contain enough naringin to inhibit the metabolism of substrates

Grapefruit is an excellent source of many nutrients and phytochemicals that contribute to a healthy diet. Grapefruit is a good source of vitamin C, contains the fibre pectin, and the pink and red hues contain the beneficial antioxidant lycopene. Studies have shown grapefruit helps lower cholesterol, and there is evidence that the seeds have antioxidant properties. Grapefruit forms a core part of the "grapefruit diet", the theory being that the fruit's low glycemic index is able to help the body's metabolism burn fat.

Grapefruit seed extract (GSE) has been shown to have strong antimicrobial properties against fungi. It is also believed to have antimicrobial properties for bacteria, however there are no known studies that demonstrate its efficacy. Additionally, although GSE is promoted as a highly effective plant-based preservative by some natural personal care manufacturers, studies have shown that the apparent antimicrobial activity associated with GSE preparations is merely due to contamination with synthetic preservatives.

Since grapefruit juice is known to inhibit enzymes necessary for the clearance of some drugs and hormones, some have hypothesized that grapefruit juice may play an indirect role in the development of hormone-dependent cancers. A 2007 study found a correlation between eating a quarter of grapefruit daily and a 30 per cent increase in risk for breast cancer in post-menopausal women. The study points to the inhibition of CYP3A4 enzyme by grapefruit, which metabolizes estrogen. However, a 2008 study has shown that grapefruit consumption does not increase breast cancer risk and found a significant decrease in breast cancer risk with greater intake of grapefruit in women who never used hormone therapy.

Grapefruit contains large quantities of a simple polyamine called spermidine, which may be related to aging. It is known to be necessary for cell growth and maturation, and as cells age their level of spermidine is known to fall. Scientists have shown that feeding spermidine to worms, fruit flies and yeast significantly prolongs their lifespan. In addition, adding spermidine to the diet of mice decreased molecular markers of aging, and when human immune cells were cultured in a medium containing spermidine, they also lived longer.

Nutritional Information

100g of grapefruit contains the following nutritional information according to the USDA

- Calories: 32
- Fat: 0.10
- Carbohydrates: 8.08
- Fibres: 1.1
- Protein: 0.63
- Cholesterol: 0

An early pioneer in the American citrus industry was Kimball Chase Atwood, a wealthy entrepreneur who founded the Atwood Grapefruit Co. in the late 19th century. The Atwood Grove became the largest grapefruit grove in the world, with an annual production of 80,000 boxes of fruit. It was there that pink grapefruit was first discovered in 1906.

Guava Fruit

Guava fruit, usually 4 to 12 centimetres (1.6 to 4.7 in) long, are round or oval depending on the species. The outer skin may be rough, often with a bitter taste, or soft and sweet. Varying between species, the skin can be any thickness, is usually green before maturity, but becomes yellow, maroon, or green when ripe.

Guava fruit generally have a pronounced and typical fragrance, similar to lemon rind but less sharp. Guava pulp may be sweet or sour, tasting something between pear and strawberry, off-white ("white" guavas) to deep pink ("red" guavas), with the seeds in the central pulp of variable number and hardness, depending on species.

Guavas are cultivated in many tropical and subtropical countries. Several species are grown commercially; apple guava and its cultivars are those most commonly traded internationally.

Guavas are also of interest to home growers in temperate areas. They are one of the few tropical fruits that can grow to fruiting size in pots indoors. When grown from seed, guavas can bear fruit as soon as two years, or as long as eight years.

In Hawaii, guava is eaten with soy sauce and vinegar. Occasionally, a pinch of sugar and black pepper are added to the mixture. The fruit is cut up and dipped into the sauce.

In Mexico, the Agua fresca beverage is popularly made with Guava. The entire fruit is a key ingredient in punch, and the juice extract is often used in culinary sauces (hot or cold), as well as artisan candies, dried snacks, fruit bars, desserts, or dipped in Chamoy. *Pulque de Guava* is a popular blend of the native alcoholic beverage.

In Pakistan and India, guava is often eaten raw, typically cut into quarters with a pinch of salt and pepper and sometimes cayenne powder/masala. Street vendors often sell guava fruit for a few rupees each.

In the Philippines, ripe guava is used in cooking sinigang

Guava juice is very popular in Cuba, Costa Rica, Egypt, Mexico, Colombia, Hawaii, Puerto Rico, Venezuela, and South Africa.

The fruit is also often prepared as a dessert, in fruit salads. In Asia, fresh guava slices are often dipped in preserved prune powder or salt. In India it is often sprinkled with red rock salt, which is very tart.

Because of its high level of pectin, guavas are extensively used to make candies, preserves, jellies, jams, and marmalades (such as Brazilian *goiabada* and Colombian *bocadillo*), and also for juices and aguas frescas.

"Red" guavas can be used as the base of salted products such as sauces, substituting for tomatoes, especially for those sensitive to the latter's acidity. In Asia, a drink is made from an infusion of guava fruits and leaves. In Brazil, the infusion made with guava tree leaves (chá-de-goiabeira, i.e. "tea" of guava tree leaves) is considered medicinal.

Guavas are rich in dietary fibre, vitamins A and C, folic acid, and the dietary minerals, potassium, copper and manganese. Having a generally broad, low-calorie profile of essential nutrients, a single common guava (*P. guajava*) fruit contains about four times the amount of vitamin C as an orange.

However, nutrient content varies across guava cultivars. Although the strawberry guava (*P. littorale* var. *cattleianum*), notably containing 90 mg of vitamin C per serving, has about 25 per cent of the amount found in more common varieties, its total vitamin C content in one serving still provides 100 per cent of the Dietary Reference Intake for adult males.

Guavas contain both carotenoids and polyphenols like (+)-gallocatechin, guaijaverin, leucocyanidin and amritoside the major classes of antioxidant pigments – giving them relatively high potential antioxidant value among plant foods. As these pigments produce the fruit skin and flesh colour, guavas that are red-orange have more pigment content as polyphenol, carotenoid and pro-vitamin A, retinoid sources than yellow-green ones.

Potential Medical Uses

Since the 1950s, guavas – particularly the leaves – have been the subject for diverse research on their constituents, pharmacological properties and history in folk medicine. Most research, however, has been conducted on apple guava (*P. guajava*), with other species remaining unstudied. From preliminary medical research in laboratory models, extracts from apple guava leaves or bark are implicated in therapeutic mechanisms against cancer, bacterial infections, inflammation and pain. Essential oils from guava leaves display anti-cancer activity *in vitro*.

Guava leaves are used in folk medicine as a remedy for diarrhea and, as well as the bark, for their supposed antimicrobial properties and as an astringent. Guava leaves or bark are used in traditional treatments against diabetes. In Trinidad, a tea made from young leaves is used for diarrhoea, dysentery and fever.

CHAPTER 10

Jackfruit

The jackfruit (*Artocarpus heterophyllus*) is a species of tree in the *Artocarpus* genus of the mulberry family (*Moraceae*). It is native to parts of South and Southeast Asia, and is believed to have originated in the southwestern rain forests of India, in present-day Kerala and coastal Karnataka. This tree is widely cultivated in tropical regions of India, Bangladesh, Sri Lanka, Vietnam, Thailand, Malaysia, Indonesia and the Philippines. Jackfruit is also found in East Africa, e.g., in Uganda and Mauritius, as well as throughout Brazil and Caribbean nations such as Jamaica.

The jackfruit tree is well suited to tropical lowlands, and its fruit is the largest tree-borne fruit, reaching as much as 80 pounds (36 kg) in weight and up to 36 inches (90 cm) long and 20 inches (50 cm) in diametre.

The word "jackfruit" comes from Portuguese *jaca*, which in turn, is derived from the Malayalam language term, *chakka* (Malayalam:). When the Portuguese arrived in India at Kozhikode (Calicut) on the Malabar Coast (Kerala) in 1498, the Malayalam name *chakka* was recorded by Hendrik van Rheede (1678-1703) in the *Hortus Malabaricus*, vol. iii in Latin Henry Yule translated the book in Jordanus Catalani's (1678-1703) *Mirabilia Descripta: The Wonders of the East*.

The common English name "jackfruit" was used by the physician and naturalist Garcia de Orta in his 1563 book *Colóquios dos simples e drogas da India*. Centuries later, botanist Ralph Randles Stewart suggested it was named after William Jack (1795-1822), a Scottish botanist who worked for the East India Company in Bengal, Sumatra and Malaysia. This is apocryphal, as the fruit was called a "jack" in English before William Jack was born: for instance, in Dampier's 1699 book, *A New Voyage Round the World*.

The jackfruit has played a significant role in Indian agriculture for centuries. Archeological findings in India have revealed jackfruit was cultivated in India 3000 to 6000 years ago.

The jackfruit is considered an invasive species in Brazil, especially in the Tijuca Forest National Park in Rio de Janeiro. The Tijuca forest is mostly an artificial secondary forest, whose planting began during the mid-19th century, and jackfruit trees have been a part of the park's flora since its founding. Recently, the species expanded excessively because its fruits, once they had naturally fallen to the ground and opened, were eagerly eaten by small mammals such as the common marmoset and the coati. The seeds are dispersed by these animals, which allows the jackfruit to compete for space with native tree species. Additionally, as the marmoset and coati also prey opportunistically on bird's eggs and nestlings, the supply of jackfruit as a ready source of food has allowed them to expand their populations, to the detriment of the local bird populations. Between 2002 and 2007, 55,662 jackfruit saplings were destroyed in the Tijuca Forest area in a deliberate culling effort by the park's management.

The flesh of the jackfruit is starchy and fibrous, and is a source of dietary fibre. The flavour is similar to a tart banana. Varieties are distinguished according to the characteristics of the fruits' flesh. In Brazil, three varieties are recognized. These are: *jaca-dura,* or "hard" variety, which has firm flesh and the largest fruits that can weigh between 15 and 40 kilograms each; *jaca-mole,* or "soft" variety, which bears smaller fruits, with softer and sweeter flesh; and *jaca-manteiga,* or "butter" variety, which bears sweet fruits, whose flesh has a consistency intermediate between the "hard" and "soft" varieties.

In Kerala, two varieties of jackfruit predominate: *varikka* and *koozha*. *Varikka* has slightly hard inner flesh when ripe, while the inner flesh of the ripe *koozha* fruit is very soft and almost dissolving. A sweet preparation called *chakka varattiyathu* (jackfruit jam) is made by seasoning the *varikka* fruit flesh pieces in jaggery, which can be preserved and used for many months. Huge jackfruits up to four feet in length with matching girth are sometimes seen in Kerala . In Mangalore, Karnataka, the varieties are called *bakke* and *imba*. The pulp of the *imba* jackfruit is ground and made into a paste, then spread over a mat and allowed to dry in the sun to create a natural chewy candy.

Jackfruit is commonly used in South and Southeast Asian cuisines. It can be eaten unripe (young) when cooked, or ripe uncooked. The seeds may be boiled or baked like beans. The leaves are used as a wrapping for steamed idlis. In Singapore, fried jackfruit is known as *cempedak goreng*.

The young fruit is called *polos* in Sri Lanka and *idichakka or idianchakka* in Kerala. It is a dish with spices to replace meat curries in Sri Lankan and eastern-Indian (Bengali) and Kerala cuisine. The skin of unripe jack fruit must be peeled first and discarded, then the whole fruit can be chopped into edible portions and cooked to be eaten. The raw young fruit is not edible. Young jackfruit has a mild flavour and distinctive poultry-like texture. The cuisines of India, Nepal, Bangladesh, Sri Lanka, Indonesia, Cambodia, and Vietnam use cooked young jackfruit. In Indonesia, young jackfruit is cooked with coconut milk as *gudeg*. In many cultures, jackfruit is boiled and used in curries as a staple food.

In the Philippines, it is cooked with coconut milk (*ginataang langka*). In Reunion Island (France), it is cooked with shrimp or smoked pork.

Ripe jackfruit is naturally sweet with subtle flavouring. It can be used to make a variety of dishes, including custards, cakes, *halo-halo* and more. Ripe jackfruit arils are sometimes seeded, fried or freeze-dried and sold as jackfruit chips.

Seeds from ripe fruits are edible and are prepared by boiling in salted water for about 25 minutes. They have a milky, sweet taste. In many parts of India, roasted salted seed is also eaten and considered a delicacy.

The wood of the tree is used for the production of musical instruments. In Indonesia, hardwood from the trunk is carved out to form the barrels of drums used in the *gamelan*, and in the Philippines, its soft wood is made into the hull of a *kutiyapi*, a type of Philippine boat lute. It is also used to make the body of the Indian string instrument *veena* and the drums *mridangam* and *kanjira*; the golden yellow-coloured timber with good grains is used for building furniture and house construction in India. The ornate wooden plank called avani palaka made of the wood of jackfruit tree is used as the priest's seat during Hindu ceremonies in Kerala.

Jackfruit wood is widely used in the manufacture of furniture, doors and windows, and in roof construction. The heartwood is used by Buddhist forest monastics in Southeast Asia as a dye, giving the robes of the monks in those traditions their distinctive light-brown colour.

CHAPTER 11

Kumquat, Kiwifruit

Kumquat

Kumquats or cumquats are a group of small fruit-bearing trees in the flowering plant family Rutaceae, either forming the genus *Fortunella*, or placed within *Citrus sensu lato*. The edible fruit closely resembles that of the orange (*Citrus sinensis*), but it is much smaller and ovular, being approximately the size and shape of an olive. The English name "kumquat" derives from the Cantonese word "gam gwat".

They are slow-growing evergreen shrubs or short trees, from 2.5 to 4.5 metres (8 to 15 ft) tall, with dense branches, sometimes bearing small thorns. The leaves are dark glossy green, and the flowers white, similar to other citrus flowers, borne singly or clustered in the leaf-axils. Depending on size, the kumquat tree can produce hundreds or even thousands of fruits each year. The tree can be hydrophytic, with the fruit often found floating on water near shore during the ripe season.

The plant is native to south Asia and the Asia-Pacific region. The earliest historical reference to kumquats appears in literature of China in the 12th century. They have long been cultivated in Japan, Taiwan, the Philippines, and southeast Asia. They were introduced to Europe in 1846 by Robert Fortune, collector for the London Horticultural Society, and shortly thereafter into North America.

Round Kumquat

The round kumquat (also Marumi kumquat or Morgani kumquat) is an evergreen tree, producing edible golden-yellow coloured fruit. The fruit is small and usually round but can be oval shaped. The peel has a sweet flavor but the fruit has a sour centre. The fruit can be eaten cooked but is mainly used to make marmalade and jelly. It is grown as an ornamental plant and can be used in bonsai. This plant symbolizes good luck in China and other Asian countries, where it is sometimes given as a gift during the Lunar New Year. It's more commonly cultivated than most other kumquats as it is cold tolerant. It can be kept as a houseplant.

When the kumquats are divided into multiple species the name *Fortunella japonica* (*Citrus japonica*) is retained by this group.

Oval Kumquat

Fortunella margarita, also known as the oval kumquat or the Nagami kumquat, is a close relative to Citrus species. It is a small evergreen tree, that can reach more than 12 ft (4 m) high and 9 ft (3 m) large. It is native to southeastern Asia, and more precisely to China. The oval kumquat has very fragrant citrus-like white flowers, and small edible oval orange fruits. The oval kumquat is an ornamental little tree, with showy foliage, flowers and fruits. It is also fairly frost-hardy, and will withstand negative temperatures such as 14 °F (-10 °C), and even a little lower for very brief periods. It can be grown in USDA hardiness zones 9 and warmer, but can also be tried in sheltered places, in USDA hardiness zone 8. Unlike most citrus species, the oval kumquat has a shorter growth period, and goes into dormancy fairly earlier in autumn. This partly explains its better frost hardiness.

Characteristics

The evergreen leaves of the oval kumquat are deep-green and relatively small. They can reach up to 3 in (7 cm) long and 1.5 in (3.5 cm) wide. The white flowers of the oval kumquat are similar to the citrus flowers. They are strongly perfumed, and they appear relatively late in the growing season, generally late spring.

The oval kumquat is a fruit that looks like any citrus fruit, with an orange rind. The fruits are oblong, up to 2 in (5 cm) long. Unlike the common citrus, which have a rind which is inedible raw, oval kumquats have an edible sweet rind. The flesh, however, is not as sweet as the rind, and the juice is quite acidic and sour, with a lemon-like flavor. This fruit is generally eaten fresh, with its rind. It can also be processed into preserves, jams, and other products.

Cultivation

The oval kumquat needs a well-drained and fertile ground. It dislikes alkaline soils. The oval kumquat is susceptible to common citrus pests and diseases.

Jiangsu Kumquat

The Jiangsu kumquat or Fukushu kumquat bears edible fruit that can be eaten raw. The fruit can be made into jelly and marmalade. The fruit can be round or bell shaped, it's bright orange when fully ripe. It may also be distinguished from other kumquats by its round leaves that make this species unique within the genus. It is grown for its edible fruit and as an ornamental plant. It cannot withstand frost

When the kumquats are divided into multiple species the name *Fortunella obovata* (*Citrus obovata*) is used for this group.

Kumquats are often eaten raw. As the rind is sweet and the juicy centre is sour, the raw fruit is usually consumed either whole—to savour the contrast—or only the rind is eaten. The fruit is considered ripe when it reaches a yellowish-orange stage and has just shed the last tint of green.

Culinary uses include candying and kumquat preserves, marmalade, and jelly. Kumquats can also be sliced and added to salads. In recent years kumquats have gained popularity as a garnish for cocktail beverages, including the martini as a replacement for the more familiar olive. A kumquat liqueur mixes the fruit with vodka or other clear spirit. Kumquats are also being used by chefs to create a niche for their desserts and are common in European countries.

The Cantonese often preserve kumquats in salt or sugar. A batch of the fruit is buried in dry salt inside a glass jar. Over time, all the juice from the fruit is diffused into the salt. The fruit in the jar becomes shrunken, wrinkled, and dark brown in colour, and the salt combines with the juice to become a dark brown brine. A few salted kumquats with a few teaspoons of the brine/juice may be mixed with hot water to make a remedy for sore throats. A jar of such preserved kumquats can last several years and still keep its flavor.

In the Philippines and Taiwan, kumquats are a popular addition to green tea and black tea, either hot or iced.

In Vietnam, kumquat bonsai trees (round kumquat plant) are used as a decoration for the (Lunar New Year) holiday.

Variants of the kumquat are grown specially in India.

Hybrid forms of the kumquat include the following:

- Limequat - key lime + kumquat
- Orangequat - Satsuma mandarin + kumquat
- Calamondin - tangerine + kumquat
- Citrangequat - citrange + kumquat
- Mandarinquat - mandarin + kumquat
- Procimequat - limequat + kumquat
- Sunquat - lemon + kumquat
- Yuzuquat - yuzu + kumquat

Hong Kong or Chin Chu

Hong Kong varieties are also called as chin chü, shan chin kan, and chin tou that belongs to the native Hong Kong and adjacent hilly and mountainous regions of Kwantung and Chekiang Provinces of China.

It is around 1.6-2 cm wide and the peel is orange in colour or scarlet when mature.

- The pulp of this fruit contains only 3 or 4 small segments.

- Chinese people flock to the foothills to collect these fruits.
- In the western world, the thorny shrub is grown only as an ornamental pot plant.

Marumi or Round Kumquat

- 'Marumi'or Round Kumquat are accounted by the first time in 1784 and introduced into Florida by Glen St from Japan.
- The 'Marumi' is also known as 'Calamondin' kumquat that are flattened, like mini mandarins.
- The fruit of this plant is round in shape, slightly oblate or obovate to 1¼ in (3.2 cm).
- It is long and the peel is golden-yellow in colour with smooth texture containing larger oil glands
- Marumi trees fruit several times a year, with the main crop in winter.
- The bushes are dense and they are the best looking of all citrus in containers and reaches 9 ft (2.75 m).

Meiwa or Large Round Kumquat

- 'Meiwa' or Large Round are also called as ninpo or neiha kinkan
- This fruit is a hybrid between 'Nagami' and 'Marumi' was introduced from Japan by the U.S Department of Agriculture in 1910-1912.
- It is short-oblong to round, about 1½ in (4 cm) wide and the peel is orange-yellow in colour.
- The pulp usually have 7 segments, relatively sweet or subacid and are often seedless or with few seeds.
- The tree is dwarf, frequently thornless or having short, stout spines.
- The leaves of this tree are very thick and rigid and partly folded lengthwise and are pitted with numerous dark-green oil glands.

Nordmann Seedless Kumquat

- This Fruit was discovered on a Nagami seedling by George Otto Nordmann in 1965.
- This fruit is similar to Nagami, slightly differ in shape with lighter skin and contains no seeds.
- This fruit is medium in size with teardrop shape, and hence it is tapered towards at the end of the stem.
- This fruit is rind thick, yellow-orange in colour.
- The pulp of this fruit is tart and are fairly juicy.
- The flavor of this fruit is similar to Nagami and it is seedless fruit.
- This fruit commercially grown in very small quantities in California.

Nagami or Oval Kumquat

'Nagami', or Oval Kumquat plants are introduced from China to London in 1846 by Robert Fortune, plant explorer for the Royal Horticultural Society was reported in North America in 1850.

This plant is obovate or oblong up to $1^3/_4$ in (4.5 cm) long and $1^3/_{16}$ in (3 cm) wide.

The pulp of this fruit can be divided into 4 or 5 segments, contains 2 to 5 seeds.

The Nagami Kumquat fruit stays fresh on the tree longer.

This trees can withstand temperatures as low as 28F which make it easily grown in areas that are too cold for most varieties of citrus.

Kumquats are low in calories. 100 g of fresh fruit contain only 71 calories. They are incredibly rich sources of health benefiting dietary fibre. The minerals, vitamins, and anti-oxidants present in this fruit contribute immense benefits to our health and wellness.

Kumquats can be eaten along with the peel contains unique feature that differentiates them from other citrus family fruits. The peel is rich in essential oils, anti-oxidants, and fibre. 100 g kumquats provide 17 per cent recommended levels of of tannins, pectin, hemi-cellulose, and other non-starch polysaccharides.

Fresh fruits contain adequate levels of anti-oxidant vitamins such as vitamin A, C and E. These phyto-chemical compounds in kumquat fruit helps scaverge harmful oxygen derived free radicals from the body and thereby protect us from cancers, diabetes, degenerative diseases and infections.

Kumquats also very rich in vitamin C. Vitamin C is one of powerful natural anti-oxidant which has many essential biological roles like collagen synthesis and wound healing; anti-viral, anti-cancer activity and helps prevent from neuro-degenerative diseases, arthritis, diabetes, etc. by removing oxidant free-radicals from the body.

Kumquats contain good levels of B-complex group of vitamins such as thiamin, niacin, pyridoxine, folates and pantothenic acid. These vitamins function for metabolism of carbohydrates, proteins, and fats.

It also contains minerals like calcium, copper, potassium, manganese, iron, selenium and zinc. Potassium is an important component of cell and body fluids that helps controlling heart rate and blood pressure. Copper is required in the production of red blood cells. Iron is required for red blood cell formation as well for cellular oxidation.

Kiwifruit

The kiwifruit, or often shortened to kiwi in many parts of the world, is the edible berry of a cultivar group of the woody vine *Actinidia deliciosa* and hybrids between this and other species in the genus *Actinidia*.

The most common cultivars of kiwifruit are oval, about the size of a large hen's egg (5-8 cm/2-3 in long and 4.5-5.5 cm/1¾-2 in diameter). It has a fibrous, dull brown-green skin and bright green or golden flesh with rows of tiny, black, edible seeds. The fruit has a soft texture and a sweet but unique flavor, and today is a commercial crop in several countries, such as Italy, New Zealand, Chile, Greece and France.

Also known as the Chinese gooseberry, the fruit was renamed for export marketing reasons in the 1950s; briefly to *melonette*, and then later by New Zealand exporters to *kiwifruit*. The name "kiwifruit" comes from the kiwi — a brown flightless bird and New Zealand's national symbol. Kiwi is also a colloquial name for New Zealanders.

Kiwifruit is a rich source of vitamin C, 1.5 times the DRI scale in the U.S. per 100 grams. Its potassium content by weight is slightly less than that of a banana. It also contains vitamin E, and a small amount of vitamin A. The skin is a good source of flavonoid antioxidants (though it may also retain agricultural pesticides. The kiwifruit seed oil contains on average 62 per cent alpha-linolenic acid, an omega-3 fatty acid. Usually a medium size kiwifruit contains about 46 calories, 0.3 g fat, 1 g protein, 11 g carbohydrates, and 2.6 g dietary fibre found partly in the edible skin. Kiwifruit is often reported to have mild laxative effects, due to its significant levels of dietary fibre.

Raw kiwifruit is also rich in the protein-dissolving enzyme actinidin, (in the same family of thiol proteases as papain), which is commercially useful as a meat tenderizer, but can be an allergen for some individuals. Specifically, people allergic to latex, bananas, papayas or pineapples are likely to also be allergic to kiwifruit. The fruit also contains calcium oxalate crystals in the form of raphides. Reactions to these chemicals include sweating, tingling and sore mouth or throat; swelling of the lips, tongue and face; rash; vomiting and abdominal pain, heartburn; and, in the most severe cases, breathing difficulties, wheezing and collapse. The most common symptoms are unpleasant itching and soreness of the mouth, with the most common severe symptom being wheezing. Severe symptoms are most likely to occur in young children.

Actinidin also makes raw kiwifruit unsuitable for use in desserts containing milk or any other dairy products which are not going to be served within hours, because the enzyme soon begins to digest milk proteins. This applies to gelatin-based desserts as well, as the actinidin will dissolve the collagen proteins in gelatin very quickly, either liquifying the dessert, or preventing it from solidifying. However, the U.S. Department of Agriculture suggests cooking the fruit for a few minutes before adding it to the gelatin to overcome this effect. Sliced kiwifruit has long been regularly used as a garnish atop whipped cream on New Zealand's national dessert, the pavlova. It can also be used in curry.

Kiwifruit components, possibly involving vitamin E and omega-3 fatty acids from its numerous edible seeds, have potential properties of a natural blood thinner. A study performed at the University of Oslo in Norway reported consuming two to three kiwifruit daily for 28 days significantly reduced platelet aggregation and blood triglyceride levels (similar to popular mainstream aspirin therapy), potentially reducing the risk of blood clots.

Kiwi fruit are called as Chinese Gooseberry, but now it is known as the kiwi fruit. It was introduced into New Zealand in 1906 from China, where it originated, and has been commercially cultivated there ever since. The kiwi Fruit, often called askiwi in many parts of the world It is the edible berry belongs to the group woody vine *Actinidia deliciosa* and genus *Actinidia*.The fruit has a soft texture and sweet in taste.Today the commercial crop in several countries, such as Italy, New Zealand, Chile, Greece and France are only the kiwi fruit.

Protective effects were found after a study on a sample of children aged 6-7 years who consumed kiwi fruit, reducing the risk of respiratory problems. They have reduced the number of episodes of wheezing by 44 per cent, compared with other children. The benefits of kiwi fruit were very obvious in children with asthma and protective effects were observed in those who consumed even one fruit a week.

Heart and Colon Health

As the kiwi fruit is rich in fibre, it reduces waste cholesterol and the risk of cardiovascular disease, and also removes toxins from the colon and helps in preventing colon cancer. The foods high in fibre are recommended for people with diabetes, as these can maintain the normal glucose level.

Age Related Muscular Degeneration (ARMD)

Considers cherries among the very most healthful and nutritious foods you can eat. Aside from being a good source of vitamin A, Dr. Bowden explains that cherries contain two valuable cancer-fighting compounds, quercetin and ellagic acid. Quercetin is a powerful antioxidant that destroys free radicals and also exhibits anti-inflammatory capabilities that may help to prevent heart disease. According to Dr. Bowden, ellagic acid can inhibit the growth of cancer cells and may even directly kill existing cancer cells without affecting your healthy cells.

It is important to note that kiwi fruits contain a remarkable amount of Vitamin C, E and A. Vitamin C is a water-soluble antioxidant that has been proven to protect our body from free radicals, dramatically improving the health of individuals who consumed it regularly against all kinds of disease, from cardiovascular problems to cancer and obesity. Vitamin E has been proven to have similar effects, but is fat-soluble and thus is complimentary to Vitamin C in its functions. Kiwi fruits contain both these vitamins in high amount, which help protect our body against free radicals from all fronts.

Cardiovascular Disease

This means heart health, including blood vessels. Taking an aspirin everyday has been recommended by doctors to help thin the blood. No need to damage other parts of your body by taking a drug every day. Kiwifruit is a natural blood thinner.In tests using 2-3 kiwifruit a day, it was shown to lower a person's triglyceride levels by 15 per cent. Triglycerides are fats in your blood which we get from unhealthy animal fats and trans fats from processed foods. A build up of these fats are what can lead to heart attacks. The other positive thing from this was kiwifruit also reduced platelet aggregation by 18 per cent. This is "stickiness" that forms in the blood which can lead to poor circulation, taxing the heart.

Constipation

One of the reasons of constipation is fecal residue in food and water. Although Fruits are rich in dietary can not be digested and absorbed soon, but it can absorb and retain moisture, so that faces become soft; also stimulates the secretion of digestive juice and intestinal peristalsis, is conducive to the stool excretion, play a role in the prevention and treatment of constipation. More fruit with fibre in the treatment of constipation are kiwi, watermelon, bananas, grapefruit, and orange, and jujube, mulberry and so on. kiwi contains more dietary fibre and oligosaccharides, protein enzymes, rapid clearance of these substances in the body in addition to the harmful accumulation of metabolites, prevention, treatment of constipation, there are very good role in preventing colon cancer and atherosclerosis.

CHAPTER 12

Lemon, Lime (Fruit), Lychee

Lemon

The lemon is both a small evergreen tree (*Citrus × limon*, often given as *C. limon*) native to Asia, and the tree's ellipsoidal yellow fruit. The fruit is used for culinary and non-culinary purposes throughout the world – primarily for its juice, though the pulp and rind (zest) are also used, mainly in cooking and baking. Lemon juice is about 5 per cent to 6 per cent (approximately 0.3 M) citric acid, which gives lemons a sour taste, and a pH of 2-3. Many lemon flavored drinks and foods are available, including lemonade and sherbet lemons, as well as lemon and seasoning salt as a snack. The distinctive sour taste of lemon juice makes it a key ingredient in many dishes across the world.

The exact origin of the lemon has remained a mystery, though it is widely presumed that lemons first grew in Southern India, northern Burma, and China. In South and South East Asia, it was known for its antiseptic properties and it was used as an antidote for various poisons. Lemons entered Europe (near southern Italy) no later than the 1st century AD, during the time of Ancient Rome. However, they were not widely cultivated. It was later introduced to Persia and then to Iraq and Egypt around AD 700. The lemon was first recorded in literature in a 10th century Arabic treatise on farming, and was also used as an ornamental plant in early Islamic gardens. It was distributed widely throughout the Arab world and the Mediterranean region between 1000 and 1150.

In India, Lemon is used in day to day life for various purposes. It is used in all Indian traditional medicines mainly in Siddha Medicine and Ayurveda. It is one of the main ingredients in many of the Indian cuisines. Either lemon pickle or mango pickle is part of everyday lunch meal in Southern India. In Hindu Pooja, lemon takes a very important place.

The first substantial cultivation of lemons in Europe began in Genoa in the middle of the 15th century. It was later introduced to the Americas in 1493 when Christopher Columbus brought lemon seeds to Hispaniola along his voyages. Spanish conquest throughout the New World helped spread lemon seeds. It was mainly used as ornament and medicine. In the 18th and 19th centuries, when lemons were first used widely in cooking and flavoring, they were increasingly planted in Florida and California.

In 1747, James Lind's experiments on seamen suffering from scurvy involved adding vitamin C to their diets with lemon juice.

The etymological path of the word lemon suggests a Middle Eastern origin. One of the earliest occurrences of "lemon" appears in a Middle English customs document of 1420-1421, which draws from the Old French *limon*, thence the Italian *limone*, from the Arabic *laymun* or *limun* , and from the Persian *limun* (a generic term for the fruit of this kind) which is congnative with Sanskrit (nimbu, "lime").

It has been suggested that lemons, limes and sour orange are mutations of the citron. A recent study of the genetic origin of the lemon, however, reports that it is a hybrid between sour orange and citron.

Growing Lemons

Lemons, in common with other sweeter, slow growing varieties of citrus, often benefit from being grafted to more vigorous rootstocks.

Differences Between Orange and Lemon

Various citruses do not fit the popular or botanical definition of oranges or lemons. For instance the kratta citrus of India has an orange leaf, an orange exterior, an orange pulp, yet its fruit is prominently mammillate (covered with rounded protuberances), and its flower is tinged purple. The acidless citrus, the *mitha-nimboo*, has a lemon-yellow exterior, a white pulp, and it is mammillate. Its leaves are like a lemon's, but its flowers are pure white. The jhambiri proper has orange-like leaves, the flowers are slightly tinged with purple, the pulp, varies from white to pale yellow, or orange, and the fruit is mammillate, and of two kinds externally, either of an orange colour, or of a lemon-yellow, and possibly also of a fawn colour.

Varieties

Bonnie Brae

Oblong, smooth, thin skinned and seedless; mostly grown in San Diego County.

Bush Lemon Tree

This naturalized lemon grows wild in subtropical Australia. It is very hardy, and has a thick skin with a true lemon flavor; the zest is good for cooking. It grows to about 4m in a sunny position.

Eureka

Because it grows year-round and abundantly, this is the common supermarket lemon.

Femminello St. Teresa, or *Sorrento* Native to Italy, this fruit's zest is high in lemon oils. It is the variety traditionally used in the making of limoncello.

Jhambiri C. *jhambiri* (Tan) The Rough lemon has a lemon yellow exterior and a very sour pulp. It is widely used as a rootstock in S. Asia.

Lisbon

A good quality bitter lemon with high juice and acid levels, the fruits of Lisbon are very similar to Eureka. The vigorous and productive trees are very thorny, particularly when young.

This is a cross between a lemon and possibly an orange or a mandarin, and was named for Frank N. Meyer, who first discovered it in 1908. Thin-skinned and slightly less acidic than the Lisbon and Eureka lemons, Meyer lemons require more care when shipping and are not widely grown on a commercial basis. Meyer lemons have a much thinner rind, and often mature to a yellow-orange colour. Meyer lemons are slightly more frost-tolerant than other lemons.

Ponderosa

The tree is more cold-sensitive than true lemons; the fruit are thick-skinned and very large. Likely a citron-lemon hybrid.

Variegated Pink

A varietal of the eureka or lisbon cultivars with variegated patterns in the foliage and the rinds of immature green fruit. Upon maturing to yellow, the variegated pattern recedes in the fruit rind. The flesh and juice are pink or pinkish-orange instead of yellow.

Verna

A Spanish variety of unknown origin.

Villafranca

Originated in China and later introduced to Japan and Korea, yuzu have a flavor akin to a mixture of meyer lemon and white grapefruit. Yuzu is likely a wild hybrid between an ichang papeda and a sour mandarin, and is a close relative of sudachi and kaffir limes. Yuzu rival citranges and kumquats as the most cold-tolerant citrus.

The average lemon contains approximately 3 tablespoons (50 mL) of juice. Allowing lemons to come to room temperature before squeezing (or heating briefly in a microwave) makes the juice easier to extract. Lemons left unrefrigerated for long periods of time are susceptible to mold.

Lemon juice, rind, and zest are used in a wide variety of culinary applications:

- Lemon juice is used to make lemonade, soft drinks, cocktails, and marinades for both fish, where its acid neutralizes amines in fish by converting them into non-volatile ammonium salts, and meat, where the acid partially hydrolyzes tough collagen fibres, tenderizing the meat, but the low pH denatures the proteins, causing them to dry out when cooked. Lemon juice is frequently used in the United Kingdom to add to pancakes, especially on Shrove Tuesday.

  Lemon juice is also used as a short-term preservative on certain foods that tend to oxidize and turn brown after being sliced, such as apples, bananas and avocados, where its acid denatures the enzymes that cause browning and degradation. Lemon juice and rind are used to make marmalade and lemon liqueur.
- Lemon slices and lemon rind are used a garnish for both food and drinks.
- Lemon zest, the grated outer rind of the fruit, is used to add flavor to baked goods, puddings, rice and other dishes
- Pickled lemons are a Moroccan delicacy.

Lemon leaves can be used to make a tea or preparing cooked meats and seafoods. For better taste older, dark-green leaves are suggested. The lemon tea also can serve a medicinal purpose. Lemon leaves are considered to be helpful as an anti-inflammatory agent and aid to digestion or in reducing fevers and cramps. The lemon leaf tea also acts as a cough medicine.

Non-Culinary Uses

Aromatherapy, First Aid and Medicine

In one of the most comprehensive scientific investigations done yet, researchers at The Ohio State University revealed lemon oil aroma used in aromatherapy does not influence the human immune system, but may enhance mood.

The low pH of juice makes it antibacterial.

Commercial Use

Lemons were the primary commercial source of citric acid prior to the development of fermentation-based processes.

A halved lemon is used as a finger moistener for those counting large amounts of bills, such as tellers and cashiers.

Household Use

The peel oil is used as a wood cleaner and polish, where the solvent property of *d*-limonene is employed to dissolve old wax, fingerprints, and grime.

A halved lemon dipped in salt or baking powder can be used to brighten copper cookware. The acid dissolves the tarnish and the abrasives assist the cleaning.

As a sanitary kitchen deodorizer the juice can deodorize, remove grease, bleach stains, and disinfect; when mixed with baking soda, it can remove stains from plastic food storage containers.

Insecticide

The *d*-limonene in lemon oil is used as a nontoxic insecticide treatment.

Science Education

A popular science experiment in schools involves attaching electrodes to a lemon and using it as a battery to produce electricity. Although very low power, several lemon batteries can power a small digital watch. These experiments also work with other fruits and vegetables.

Lemon juice is sometimes used as an acid in educational science experiments.

Lemon Alternatives

Many plants are noted to taste or smell similar to lemons.

- Certain cultivars of basil
- Cymbopogon (lemon grass)
- Lemon balm, a mint-like herbaceous perennial in the Lamiaceae family

- Two varieties of scented geranium: *Pelargonium crispum* (lemon geranium) and *Pelargonium × melissinum* 'Lemon Balm'

Lemongrass

Lemon myrtle, recently, this Australian bush food has become a popular alternative to lemons. The crushed and dried leaves and edible essential oils have a strong, sweet lemon taste, but contain no citric acid. Lemon myrtle is popular in foods that curdle with lemon juice, such as cheesecake and ice cream.

- Lemon thyme
- Lemon verbena
- Limes, another common sour citrus fruit, used similarly to lemons
- Certain cultivars of mint
- Magnolia grandiflora tree flowers

Person Whom May Consume Lemon

Cancer

Lemon juice is quite astringent; it is also very refreshing, high in vitamin C and contains compounds that may help prevent cancer. It helps to fight with cancer attacking cells by freeing the radicals

Diabetic

For a fruit that is difficult to enjoy by it, lemon has often contributed another dimension to food as well as a form of digestive aid. In fact, many acidic ingredients found among common household ingredients are often a practical and hassle-free means of helping diabetics deal with the problems that arise from decreased stomach acid and digestive enzymes.

Lemon juice works particularly well. As a ubiquitous fruit found in every country and sold for very little, squeezing lemon juice into one's beverage is an easy and obtainable solution to help your food digest smoothly and balance your digestive system so that it won't go into overdrive when processing difficult foods, such as carbs and fats. Here are a few easy tactics in using lemon juice and vinegar to help balance food digestion while living with diabetes.

Add lemon juice to water. A half teaspoon of lemon juice per 8 ounces of water gives you just enough to digest your food without making the water too acidic to drink. Lemon-enhanced water is perfect for diabetics, as it adds flavor without adding sugar.Take a vinegar tablet with food or in a beverage. Many diabetic companies that supply vinegar tablets have also made them flavored to help mask the bitter taste while preserving the vinegar's natural acidic qualities.

Fights Infection

Lemon is very effective in combating infections, especially in the throat as it also has antibacterial properties. For sore throat, dilute one-half with one-half water and Gargling with a 50/50 mixture of water and lemon juice frequently will get rid of many throat conditions swiftly.

Weight Loss

Drinking lemon water helps you to shed losing weight faster as well as helping to breakdown and eliminate body fat.

Eliminates Winter Blues

Lemon water is wonderful in cases of flu, fever and colds.

Cholestrol Cleanse

The Lemon is central to an effective and side-effect-free remedy for high levels of cholesterol in the body.Plaque in the arteries is a major cause of cardiovascular problems as it restricts the blood flow. The lemon and garlic cleanse takes about 6 weeks using a simple recipe and will dissolve plaque within the body. In so many cases, once the plaque begins to disappear, heart surgery is not needed.

Biliousness

In cases of drinking nothing but lemon juice and water all day cleans the system and helps overcome the biliousness.Lemon juice daily on an empty stomach first thing in the morning eliminates water retention and helps with weight reduction and keeps the system alkaline.

Diptheria

The Lemon proves the power of the strong antiseptic and digestive qualities of the fruit.The throat should be gargled with the lemon juice every hour or two.This looses the false membrane in the throat and permits it to come out."

Rheumatism

Take the juice of ½ lemon before each meal and before retiring each night mixed in water and apply the juice 2x daily externally on the sore areas.After 3 days the sure but slow power of the lemon shows it's cleansing and pain-relieving qualities.

Scurvy

The world well knows today that the lemon juice cure for scurvy is effective. There are many cases bordering on scurvy, however, showing a lack of the powerful lemon vitamins which give quick improvement in better bowel section, healing of mouth conditions, and a greater immunity to infection, when a diet very rich in vitamin C which abounds in lemon is followed.

Lime (Fruit)

Lime (from Arabic and French *lim*) is a term referring to a number of different citrus fruits, both species and hybrids, which are typically round, green to yellow in colour, 3-6 cm in diametre, and containing sour and acidic pulp. Limes are a good source of vitamin C. Limes are often used to accent the flavours of foods and beverages. Limes are grown all year round and are usually smaller and more sour than lemons.

To prevent scurvy during the 19th century, British sailors were issued a daily allowance of citrus, such as lemon, and later switched to lime, which was not as effective at preventing scurvy but was easier to obtain on Britain's Caribbean colonies. It was later discovered that the greater effectiveness of lemons derived from the 4-fold higher quantities of vitamin C lemon juice contains compared to the West Indian limes used by the British. This was initially a closely guarded military secret, as scurvy was a common enemy of various nation's navies, and being able to be at sea for lengthy periods without contracting scurvy was a huge military benefit. The British sailor acquired the nickname of being a *Limey* because of their usage of limes.

Lime juice is the juice of limes (citrus). It may be squeezed from fresh limes, or purchased in bottles in both unsweetened and sweetened varieties. Lime juice is used to make limeade, and as an ingredient (typically as sour mix) in many cocktails.

Lime extracts and essential oils are frequently used in perfumes, cleaning products, and aromatherapy.

In India, the lime is used in Tantra for removing evil spirits. It is also combined with Indian chillies to make a protective charm to repel the evil eye. Furthermore, it was believed that hanging limes over sick people cured them of the illness by repelling evil spirits lurking inside the body.

Health Effects

When the skin is exposed to ultraviolet light after lime juice contact, a reaction known as phytophotodermatitis can occur, which can cause darkening of the skin, swelling or blistering. The agent responsible for this is psoralen.

Lime contains 24 milligrams less vitamin C per 100 grams than the lemon.

Person Whom May Consume Lime

Scurvy

Lime is a cure for scurvy, which is caused due to deficiency of vitamin-C and characterized by infections such as cough and cold; cracked lips and lip corners; ulcers in tongue and mouth; spongy, swollen and bleeding gums etc. that now days even a child can tell you that. It is caused due to the deficiency of vitamin-C, its remedy is none other than vitamin-C, and lime is blessed with this vitamin. In olden days, sailors and soldiers were given lime to keep safe from scurvy, which was a dreaded disease then. It is also distributed among the workers working in polluting environments like those working in furnaces, painting shops, heat treatments, cement factories, mines etc. to protect them from scurvy.

Skin Care

Lime juice and its oil are very useful for the skin when applied orally or externally. It rejuvenates the skin, keeps it shining, protects it from infections and reduces body odor due to presence of a large amount of vitamin C and Flavonoids, both of which are class-1 anti oxidants, anti biotic and disinfectants. When applied externally on skin, its acids scrub out the dead cells, cures dandruff, rashes, bruises etc. and gives you a refreshing bath if its juice or oil is mixed into your bathing water.

Constipation

Primarily, the ample of acids present in lime helps to clear the excretory system by washing and cleaning off the tracts, just like some acids are used to clean floor and toilets. Then the roughage in it is also helpful in easing constipation. But it is mainly due to high acids. An overdose of lime juice with salt also acts as an excellent purgative without any side effects, thereby giving relief in constipation.

Peptic Ulcer and Respiratory Disorder

Due to vitamin C in lime, contains special compounds such as Flavonoids (Limonoids such as Limonin Glucoside) which have an anti oxidant, anti carcinogenic, anti biotic and detoxifying properties which help for healing of peptic and oral ulcers.Lime oil, containing Flavonoids is extensively used in anti congestive medicines such as balms, vaporizers, inhalers etc. due to the presence of Kaempferol. Just scratching the peel of a lime and inhaling it gives immediate relief in congestion and nausea.

Gout

There are two main reasons for the causes of Gout. While the first reason is accumulation of free radicals in the body and the second is accumulation of toxins, primarily the uric acid. Now, limes can help you with both of these. It is a reservoir of anti oxidants & detoxifiers (vitamin-C & Flavonoids) which free the radicals as well as detoxify the body.

Gums

Gum problems are due to deficiency of vitamin-C (Scurvy, which gives bleeding and spongy gums) and microbial growth. Sometimes, the ulcers and wounds from bones, hard objects etc. are also the causes. In all of these, limes can help you. Its vitamin-C cures scurvy, Flavonoids inhibit microbial growth and potassium and Flavonoids help heal ulcers and wounds.

Piles

Lime helps to heal up ulcers and wounds found in the digestive system and excretory system and gives relief from constipation too, it eradicates all the root causes of piles

Toothaches

A diet, high in sugar and refined foods, along with the consumption of fizzy drinks (usually high in sugar) is the greatest threat to our teeth. Mouth bacteria break sugars down into different types of acids. These acids will attack the enamel on your teeth, causing decay and erosion of the protective layer on the tooth. The enamel is broken down slowly, this process can take years, after which an excruciating pain will let you know that your tooth is deteriorating but lots of people who suffer from toothaches start taking lots of painkillers to be able to ease the toothache pain. Curing toothaches is usually a task for your dentist, but a lot can be done to relieve yourself of the pain. Vitamin C, helps to maintain both bones and teeth, kills bacteria and prevents decay. Lime is known for its high vitamin C content and prevents teeth from decaying and gums from loosening around the teeth (caused by a high sugar level in the mouth). If you start adding lime juice to a glass of water every day, this can cure toothaches and help prevent them. Reducing your intake of sugars, and snacking less in between meals, will help your teeth to stay strong. Gargling with lime juice if you have a very painful toothache is an excellent home remedy.

Lychee

The lychee (*Litchi chinensis*, and also known as the *leechi, litchi, laichi, lichu, lizhi*) is the sole member of the genus *Litchi* in the soapberry family, Sapindaceae. It is a tropical and subtropical fruit tree native to southern China and Southeast Asia, and now cultivated in many parts of the world. The fresh fruit has a "delicate, whitish pulp" with a "perfume" flavor. Since this perfumy flavor is lost in canning, the fruit is usually eaten fresh.

An evergreen tree reaching 10-28 meters tall, the lychee bears fleshy fruits that are up to 5 cm (2.0 in) long and 4 cm (1.6 in) wide. The outside of the fruit is covered by a pink-red, roughly-textured rind that is inedible but easily removed to expose a layer of sweet, translucent white flesh. Lychees are eaten in many different dessert dishes, and are especially popular in China, throughout Southeast Asia, along with South Asia and India.

The lychee is cultivated in China, Thailand, Vietnam, Japan, Bangladesh and northern India (in particular Bihar, which accounts for 75 per cent of total Indian production). South Africa and the United States (Hawaii and Florida) also have commercial lychee production.

The lychee has a history of cultivation going back as far as 2000 BC according to records in China. Cultivation began in the area of southern China, Malaysia, and Vietnam. Wild trees still grow in parts of southern China and on Hainan Island.

Litchi chinensis was described and named by French naturalist Pierre Sonnerat in his *Voyage aux Indes orientales et à la Chine, fait depuis 1774 jusqu'à 1781* (1782). There are three subspecies, determined by flower arrangement, twig thickness, fruit, and number of stamens.

Litchi chinensis subsp. *chinensis* is the only commercialized lychee. It grows wild in southern China, Bangladesh northern Vietnam, and Cambodia. It has thin twigs, flowers typically have six stamens, fruit are smooth or with protuberances up to 2 mm.

- *Litchi chinensis* subsp. *philippinensis* (Radlk.) Leenh. It is common in the wild in Philippines and Papua New Guinea and rarely cultivated. It has thin twigs, six to seven stamens, long oval fruit with spiky protuberances up to 3 mm.
- *Litchi chinensis* subsp. *javensis*. It is only known in cultivation, in Malaysia and Indonesia. It has thick twigs, flowers with seven to eleven stamens in sessile clusters, smooth fruit with protuberances up to 1 mm.
- *Litchi chinensis* is an evergreen tree that is frequently less than 10 m (33 ft) tall, sometimes reaching more than 15 m (49 ft). The bark is grey-black, the branches a brownish-red. Leaves are 10 to 25 cm (3.9 to 9.8 in) or longer, with leaflets in 2-4 pairs. Litchee have a similar foliage to the Lauraceae family likely due to convergent evolution. They are adapted by developing leaves that repel water, similar to laurophyll or lauroide leaves which are adapted to high rainfall and humidity in laurel forest habitats Flowers grow on a terminal inflorescence with many panicles on the current season's growth. The panicles grow in clusters of ten or more, reaching 10 to 40 cm (3.9 to 16 in) or longer, holding hundreds of small white, yellow, or green flowers that are distinctively fragrant.

Fruits mature in 80-112 days, depending on climate, location, and cultivar. Fruits reach up to 5 cm (2.0 in) long and 4 cm (1.6 in) wide, varying in shape from round, to ovoid, to heart-shaped. The thin, tough inedible skin is green when immature, ripening to red or pink-red, and is smooth or covered with small sharp protuberances. The skin turns brown and dry when left out after harvesting. The fleshy, edible portion of the fruit is an aril, surrounding one dark brown inedible seed that is 1 to 3.3 cm (0.39 to 1.3 in) long and .6 to 1.2 cm (0.24 to 0.47 in) wide. Some cultivars produce a high percentage of fruits with shriveled aborted seeds known as 'chicken tongues'. These fruit typically have a higher price, due to having more edible flesh.

Lychees are extensively grown in China, and also elsewhere in Brazil, South-East Asia, Pakistan, Bangladesh, India, southern Japan, and more recently in California, Hawaii, Texas, Florida, the wetter areas of eastern Australia and sub-tropical regions of South Africa, Israel and also in the states of Sinaloa and San Luis Potosí (specifically, in La Huasteca) in Mexico. They require a warm subtropical to tropical climate that is cool but also frost-free or with only very slight winter frosts not below -4°C, and with high summer heat, rainfall, and humidity. Growth is best on well-drained, slightly acidic soils rich in organic matter. A wide range of cultivars is available, with early and late maturing forms suited to warmer and cooler climates respectively. They are also grown as an ornamental tree as well as for their fruit.

Lychees are commonly sold fresh in Asian markets, and in recent years, also widely in supermarkets worldwide. The red rind turns dark brown when the fruit is refrigerated, but the taste is not affected. It is also sold canned year-round. The fruit can be dried with the rind intact, at which point the flesh shrinks and darkens. Dried lychee are often called *lychee nuts*, though, of course, they are not a real nut.

According to folklore, a lychee tree that is not producing much fruit can be girdled, leading to more fruit production.

The lychee contains on average a total 72 mg of vitamin C per 100 grams of fruit. On average nine lychee fruits would meet an adult's daily recommended Vitamin C requirement.

A cup of lychee fruit provides, among other minerals, 14 per cent Daily Value (DV) of copper, 9 per cent DV of phosphorus, and 6 per cent DV of potassium (for a 2000-calorie diet).

Like most plant-based foods, lychees are low in saturated fat and sodium and are cholesterol free. Lychees have moderate amounts of polyphenols, shown in one French study to be higher than several other fruits analyzed. On the phenolic composition, flavan-3-ol monomers and dimers were the major found compounds representing about 87.0 per cent of the phenolic compounds that declined with storage or browning. Cyanidin-3-glucoside was a major anthocyanin and represented 91.9 per cent of anthocyanins. It also declined with storage or browning. Small amounts of malvidin-3-glucoside were also found.

In traditional Chinese medicine, Lychee is known for being a fruit with "hot" properties and excessive consumption of Lychee can, in certain extreme cases, lead to fainting spells or skin rashes.

Person Whom May Consume Lychee

Cancer

Lychee fruit extract showed anticancer activities. This fruit has flavonoids in the pulp which helps to prevent fatal and lethal disease like cancer. Flavones, quercitin and kaempferol as a powerful compound in reducing the proliferation of cancer cells.

Heart Diseases

Lychee fruit is an excellent source of vitamin C. Vitamin C aids the body in fighting against cancer and heart diseases. A compound extracted from lychee called Oligonol(R) have benefits for skin through improving the blood flow to the sub dermal skin layer and protecting it from damages caused by UV light and free radicals. Oligonol(R) has also shown improved cardiovascular function, reduction of visceral fat as well as reduction of exercise fatigue.

The lychee fruit protects the body from potential heart attacks. It helps to clear out blood clots and also keeps the cells healthy. 50 per cent less chance of heart attack is seen in body that ate lychee fruit several times a week than people who don't eat lychee fruit.

Gastro-Intestinal Troubles

The seed present in this fruit is astringent and is used for intestinal troubles and to get rid the body of intestinal worms. Various parts of the lychee tree are also prescribed for mild Diarrhea, gastralgia and stomach ulcers. Lychee flesh is considered a good antacid. It is used to treat High acidity, nausea and dyspepsia.

Fight Infection

Herbal tea made by boiling the peel or bark of this fruit can boost the immune system of the human body to fight against infections such as common cold and throat ailments. Traditional healers prescribe lychee for Quinsy [a painful pus filled inflammation of the tonsils and surrounding tissues; usually due to tonsillitis].They also include the peel, tree bark, roots or flowers in their herbal formulation to treats skin eruptions due to smallpox.

Prevent Blindness

The potent compound in lychee chinensis Sonn shows promise in preventing eye and nerve damage in people with diabetes. This compound has the potential to be developed into a class of drug called Aldose reductase inhibitors. The potent antioxidant capability of polyphenol has proven beneficial for a number of health conditions.

Cold and Diet

Colds and flu can cause severe dry coughs which can be very discouraging. You don't like having these coughs throughout the day and night. Lychee's can help to treat these annoying coughs because Lychee contains little or no fat at all, you can include Lychee into your daily diet. This would mean that you can choose to consume as many Lychee's as you can without having to worry about putting on weight.

Skin Protection

Person who is suffering from acne and spots, then it is required that you have to consume Lychee as much as possible. Lychee's helps to nourish your skin of oils which can help reduce the growth of acne. This fruit refines your skin when enjoyed at no limit. Refining of the skin leads to less spots on your face.

Pain

Lychee fruit has the ability to shrink the swollen glands and relieves pain associated with it. A tea made from powdered lychee seeds is used to relieve pain, including neuralgic [nerve] pain. The Chinese uses it to treat inflammations of the genitals.

CHAPTER 13

Mandarin, Mango, Purple Mangosteen, Mulberry

Mandarin

The Mandarin orange, also known as the mandarin or mandarine (both lower-case), is a small citrus tree (*Citrus reticulata*) with fruit resembling other oranges. Mandarin oranges are usually eaten plain or in fruit salads. Specifically reddish-orange mandarin cultivars can be marketed as tangerines, but this is not a botanical classification.

The tree is more drought-tolerant than the fruit. The mandarin is tender, and is damaged easily by cold. It can be grown in tropical and subtropical areas.

The mandarin orange is a variety of the orange family. The mandarin has many names, some of which actually refer to crosses between the mandarin and another citrus fruit.

- Satsuma, a seedless variety, of which there are over 200 cultivars, such as Owari and mikan; the source of most canned mandarins, and popular as a fresh fruit due to its ease of consumption.
- Owari, a well-known Satsuma cultivar which ripens during the late fall season.
- Clementine, sometimes known as a "Christmas orange", as its peak season is December; becoming the most important commercial Mandarin orange form, have displaced mikans in many markets.

- Tangerine sometimes known as "Dancy Mandarin".
- Tangor, also called the *temple orange*, a cross between the Mandarin orange and the common sweet orange; its thick rind is easy to peel and its bright orange pulp is sour-sweet and full-flavoured.

The mandarin is easily peeled with the fingers, starting at the thick rind covering the depression at the top of the fruit, and can be easily split into even segments without squirting juice. This makes it convenient to eat, as utensils are not required to peel or cut the fruit.

Canned mandarin segments are peeled to remove the white pith prior to canning; otherwise, they turn bitter. Segments are peeled using a chemical process. First, the segments are scalded in hot water to loosen the skin; then they are bathed in a lye solution which digests the albedo and membranes. Finally, the segments undergo several rinses in plain water.

During Chinese New Year, Mandarin oranges and tangerines are considered traditional symbols of abundance and good fortune. During the two-week celebration, they are frequently displayed as decoration and presented as gifts to friends, relatives, and business associates.

Biological Characteristics

Citrus fruits are usually self-fertile (needing only a bee to move pollen within the same flower) or parthenocarpic (not needing pollination and therefore seedless, such as the satsuma).

Blossoms from the Dancy cultivar are one exception. They are self-sterile, and therefore must have a pollinator variety to supply pollen, and a high bee population to make a good crop. The fruit is oblate.

In traditional Chinese medicine, the dried peel of the fruit is used in the regulation of ch'i, and also used to treat abdominal distension, to enhance digestion, and to reduce phlegm Mandarins have also been used in ayurveda (traditional medicine of India).

In Philippines all mandarin oranges are called naranjita. It is considered to be the native of south-eastern Asia and Philippines.

Health Benefits

- Mandarin fruits are used to treat abdominal distension, to enhance digestion
- It maintains optimum health and weight loss
- Vitamin C in mandarin oranges protects sperm from genetic damage
- Mandarins have been used in ayurveda and to reduce phlegm
- Mandarin fruit is an excellent source of vitamin C and flavonoids.

Mango

The mango is a fleshy stone fruit belonging to the genus *Mangifera*, consisting of numerous tropical fruiting trees in the flowering plant family Anacardiaceae. The mango is native to the Indian subcontinent from where it spread all over the world. It is one of the most cultivated fruits of the tropical world. While other *Mangifera* species (e.g. horse mango, *M. foetida*) are also grown on a more localized basis, *Mangifera indica* – the common mango or Indian mango – is the only mango tree commonly cultivated in many tropical and subtropical regions, and its fruit is distributed essentially worldwide.

In several cultures, its fruit and leaves are ritually used as floral decorations at weddings, public celebrations and religious ceremonies.

Mango peel and sap contain urushiol, the chemical in poison ivy and poison sumac that can cause urushiol-induced contact dermatitis in susceptible people. Cross-reactions between mango contact allergens and urushiol have been observed. Those with a history of poison ivy or poison oak contact dermatitis may be most at risk for such an allergic reaction. Urushiol is also present in mango leaves and stems.

During mango's primary ripening season, it is the most common source of plant dermatitis in Hawaii.

The mango is generally sweet, although the taste and texture of the flesh varies across cultivars, some having a soft, pulpy texture similar to an overripe plum, while the flesh of others is firmer, like a cantaloupe or avocado, or may have a fibrous texture. For consumption of unripe, pickled or cooked fruit, the mango skin may be consumed comfortably, but has potential to cause contact dermatitis of the lips, gingiva or tongue in susceptible people (see above) Under-ripe mangoes can be ripened by placing them in brown paper bags. They will then keep in a plastic bag in the refrigerator for about four or five days. In ripe fruits which are commonly eaten fresh, the skin may be thicker and bitter tasting, so is typically not eaten.

Mangoes are widely used in cuisine. Sour, unripe mangoes are used in chutneys, *athanu*, pickles, or side dishes, or may be eaten raw with salt, chili, or soy sauce. A cooling summer drink called *panna* or *panha* comes from mangoes. Mango jelly made of mango pulp called *mamidi thandralu* in Telugu and *mambazha vettu* in Tamil is very popular. A dish called *mamidikaya pappu* in Telugu and *mangai paruppu* in Tamil, where mangoes are cooked with red gram *dhal* and green chillies, is served with cooked rice and clarified but raw mangoes are typically eaten fresh; however, they can have many other culinary uses. Mango lassi, a popular drink made throughout South Asia, is created by mixing ripe mangoes or mango pulp with buttermilk and sugar. Ripe mangoes are also used to make curries. *Aamras* is a popular pulp/thick juice made of mangoes with sugar or milk, and is consumed with bread, rice or *pooris*. The pulp from ripe mangoes is also used to make jam called *mangada*.

Mangoes are used in preserves such as *moramba*, *amchur* (dried and powdered unripe mango) and pickles, including a spicy mustard-oil pickle and alcohol. Ripe mangoes are often cut into thin layers, desiccated, folded, and then cut. These bars are similar to dried guava fruit bars available in some countries. The fruit is also added to cereal products such as muesli and oat granola.

Unripe mango may be eaten with *bagoong* (especially in the Philippines), fish sauce or with dash of salt. Dried strips of sweet, ripe mango (sometimes combined with seedless tamarind to form *mangorind*) are also popular. Mangoes may be used to make juices, mango nectar, and as a flavoring and major ingredient in ice cream and *sorbetes*.

Mango is used to make juices, smoothies, ice cream, fruit bars, *raspados*, *aguas frescas*, pies and sweet chili sauce, or mixed with *chamoy*, a sweet and spicy chili paste. It is popular on a stick dipped in hot chili powder and salt or as a main ingredient in fresh fruit combinations. In Central America, mango is either eaten green mixed with salt, vinegar, black pepper and hot sauce, or ripe in various forms. Toasted and ground pumpkin seed (called *pepita*) with lime and salt are the norm when eating green mangoes. Some people also add soy sauce or chili sauce.

Pieces of mango can be mashed and used as a topping on ice cream or blended with milk and ice as milkshakes. Sweet glutinous rice is flavored with coconut, then served with sliced mango as a dessert. In other parts of Southeast Asia, mangoes are pickled with fish sauce and rice vinegar. Green mangoes can be used in mango salad with fish sauce and dried shrimp. Mango with condensed milk may be used as a topping for shaved ice.

The energy value per 100 g (3.5 oz) is 250 kJ (60 kcal), and that of the apple mango is slightly higher (79 kcal per 100g). Mango contains a variety of phytochemicals and nutrients. The fruit pulp is high in prebiotic dietary fibre, vitamin C, diverse polyphenols and provitamin A carotenoids.

In mango fruit pulp, the antioxidant vitamins A and C, Vitamin B_6 (pyridoxine), folate, other B vitamins and essential nutrients, such as potassium, copper and amino acids, are present. Mango peel and pulp contain other phytonutrients, such as the pigment antioxidants – carotenoids and polyphenols – and omega-3 and -6 polyunsaturated fatty acids.

Mango peel contains pigments that may have antioxidant properties, including carotenoids, such as the provitamin A compound, beta-carotene, lutein and alpha-carotene, polyphenols such as quercetin, kaempferol, gallic acid, caffeic acid, catechins, tannins, and the unique mango xanthonoid, mangiferin, any of which may counteract free radicals in various disease processes as revealed in preliminary research. Phytochemical and nutrient content appears to vary across mango species. Up to 25 different carotenoids have been isolated from mango pulp, the densest of which was beta-carotene, which accounts for the yellow-orange pigmentation of most mango species. Peel and leaves also have significant polyphenol content, including xanthonoids, mangiferin and gallic acid.

The mango triterpene, lupeol, is an effective inhibitor in laboratory models of prostate and skin cancers. An extract of mango branch bark called Vimang, isolated by Cuban scientists, contains numerous polyphenols with antioxidant properties in vitro and on blood parameters of elderly humans.

The pigment euxanthin, known as Indian yellow, is often thought to be produced from the urine of cattle fed mango leaves; the practice is described as having been outlawed in 1908 due to malnutrition of the cows and possible urushiol poisoning. This supposed origin of euxanthin appears to rely on a single, anecdotal source, and Indian legal records do not outlaw such a practice.

The mango may be an example of an evolutionary anachronism, a fruit adapted for ecological relationship with now-extinct large mammals such as giant ground sloths or gomphotheres. Most large fleshy fruits serve the function of seed dispersal, accomplished by their consumption by large animals and excreted in their dung, ready to sprout. Since there are no extant native animals large enough to effectively disperse mango seeds in this fashion, the fruit may have co-evolved with Pleistocene megafauna. If so, the mango occupies an ecological niche similar to that of the avocado.

Digestion

Cures acidity and digestion are some of the health benefits present in mango. Mango contains an enzyme which is said to help in digestion. Esters, terpenes and aldehydes are some of the bio-active ingredients present in the mangoes, which are said to increase appetite and also improve digestion.

Cancer Hazards and Lower Cholesterol

Mango contains large amount of pectin, a soluble dietary fibre that are efficiently lowers the blood cholesterol levels. Pectin also prevents you from having prostate cancer. The portion originating from pectin combines with galectin 3 (a protein playing significant role in all stages of cancer).

Digestion

Mango eliminates problems like indigestion and acidity. Moreover the digestive enzymes in mango help in digestion naturally. The bio-active ingredients in mango like esters, terpenes and aldehydes contribute in enhancing appetite and also improve digestion.

Cures Anemia and Helps in Pregnancy

Mangoes are rich in iron, are beneficial for people suffering from anemia. Regular and adequate intake of mangoes helps to avoid anemia by increasing the blood count in the body. Mangoes are also very beneficial for pregnant woman as the iron requirement is extremely essential. Doctors often prescribe iron tablets during pregnancy. Instead you can enjoy a healthy iron rich diet with the juicy mangoes.

Cures Acne

Mangoes are related with skin enhancements. Other than bringing a glow to your face, this fruit also helps to lighten skin colour. You can easily enhance your beauty by including this fruit in your diet regularly. Mangoes treat acne effectively as they open the clogged pores of the skin. Once these pores are opened, acne formation eventually stops. Unclogging the pores of the skin can be an effective way to get rid of acne.

Brain Health

Mangoes have abundant quantities of vitamin B_6, for maintaining and improving the brain functions. These vitamins aid in the amalgamation of the major neurotransmitters that contributes in determining the mood and modification of sleeping patterns. Thereby you can be assured of a sound brain and healthy nerve functioning throughout with regular mango intake and by avoiding medicinal supplements; you can stay away from its high doses that might cause nerve damage. The Glutamine acid content in mango improves concentration and memory power.

Body Immunity

Mangoes are also rich in abundant quantities of beta-carotene a carotenoid. This element helps in enhancing the immune system of the body and makes it strong. Beta-carotene gets transformed into vitamin A eventually inside the body.Vitamin A is an antioxidant and assures you protection against the innumerable free radicals that can harm your internal system. Thus, mangoes are great choice amongst the food items in your regular diet that not only assures you a disease free life but enchants you with its magnificent taste.

Rheumatism

Take the juice of ½ lemon before each meal and before retiring each night mixed in water and apply the juice 2x daily externally on the sore areas. After 3 days the sure but slow power of the lemon shows it's cleansing and pain-relieving qualities.

Scurvy

The world well knows today that the lemon juice cure for scurvy is effective. There are many cases bordering on scurvy, however, showing a lack of the powerful lemon vitamins which give quick improvement in better bowel section, healing of mouth conditions, and a greater immunity to infection, when a diet very rich in vitamin C which abounds in lemon is followed.

Purple Mangosteen

The purple mangosteen (*Garcinia mangostana*), colloquially known simply as mangosteen, is a tropical evergreen tree believed to have originated in the Sunda Islands and the Moluccas of Indonesia. The tree grows from 7 to 25 m (20-80 ft) tall. The fruit of the mangosteen is sweet and tangy, juicy, and somewhat fibrous, with an inedible, deep reddish purple-coloured rind (exocarp) when ripe. In each fruit, the fragrant edible flesh that surrounds each seed is botanically endocarp, i.e., the inner layer of the ovary.

The purple mangosteen belongs to the same genus as the other, less widely known, mangosteens, such as the button mangosteen (*G. prainiana*) or the *charichuelo* (*G. madruno*).

A description of mangosteen was included in the *Species Plantarum* by Linnaeus in 1753.

The juvenile mangosteen fruit, which does not require fertilisation to form first appears as pale green or almost white in the shade of the canopy. As the fruit enlarges over the next two to three months, the exocarp colour deepens to darker green. During this period, the fruit increases in size until its exocarp is 6-8 centimetres in outside diameter, remaining hard until a final, abrupt ripening stage.

The subsurface chemistry of the mangosteen exocarp comprises an array of polyphenols including xanthones and tannins that assure astringency which discourages infestation by insects, fungi, plant viruses, bacteria and animal predation while the fruit is immature. Colour changes and softening of the exocarp are natural processes of ripening that indicates the fruit can be eaten and the seeds have finished developing.

Mangosteen produces a recalcitrant seed and must be kept moist to remain viable until germination. Mangosteen seeds are nucellar in origin and not the result of fertilisation; they germinate as soon as they are removed from the fruit and die quickly if allowed to dry once the developing mangosteen fruit has stopped expanding, chlorophyll synthesis slows as the next colour phase begins. Initially streaked with red, the exocarp pigmentation transitions from green to red to dark purple, indicating a final ripening stage. This entire process takes place over a period of ten days as the edible quality of the fruit peaks.

Over the days following the removal from the tree, the exocarp hardens to an extent depending upon postharvest handling and ambient storage conditions, especially relative humidity levels. If the ambient humidity is high, exocarp hardening may take a week or longer when the aril quality is peaking and excellent for consumption. However, after several additional days of storage, especially if unrefrigerated, the arils inside the fruit might spoil without any obvious external indications. Using the hardness of the rind as an indicator of freshness for the first two weeks following harvest is therefore unreliable because the rind does not accurately reveal the interior condition of the arils. If the exocarp is soft and yielding as it is when ripe and fresh from the tree, the fruit is usually good.

The edible endocarp of the mangosteen is botanically defined as an aril with the same shape and size as a tangerine 4-6 centimetres in diameter, but is white. The circle of wedge-shaped arils contains 4-8 segments, the larger ones harbouring apomictic seeds that are unpalatable unless roasted.

Often described as a subtle delicacy, the arils bear an exceptionally mild aroma, quantitatively having about 1/400th of the chemical constituents of fragrant fruits, explaining its relative mildness. The main volatile components having caramel, grass and butter notes as part of the mangosteen fragrance are hexyl acetate, hexenol and a-copaene.

On the bottom of the exocarp, raised ridges (remnants of the stigma), arranged like spokes of a wheel, correspond to the number of aril sections. Mangosteens reach fruit-bearing in as little as 5-6 years, but more typically require 8-10 years.

The aril is the part of the fruit which contains the flavor; when analyzed specifically for its nutrient content, the mangosteen aril is absent of important nutrient content.

Some mangosteen juice products contain whole fruit purée or polyphenols extracted from the inedible exocarp (rind) as a formulation strategy to add phytochemical value. The resulting juice has purple colour and astringency derived from exocarp pigments, including xanthonoids under study for potential disease amelioration effects. The potential health benefits of xanthones were debated in a four-part series in 2009.

Other authors proposed alpha-mangostin, a xanthone, could stimulate apoptosis in leukemia cells *in vitro*.

Furthermore, a possible adverse effect may occur from chronic consumption of mangosteen juice containing xanthones. A 2008 medical case report described a patient with severe acidosis, possibly attributable to a year of daily use (to lose weight, dose not described) of mangosteen juice infused with tannins.

Uses in Folk Medicine

Various parts of the plant have a history of use in folk medicine, mostly in Southeast Asia. It is reputed to have possible anti-inflammatory properties, and may have been used to treat skin infections or wounds, dysentery or urinary tract infections. Research on the phytochemistry of the plant is still inadequate to assure the safety or scientific certainty of any of these effects.

Mulberry

Mulberry are obtained from the silkworm tree belonging to the family moraceae of genus Morus. The Scientific name of this fruit is *Morus nigra* purple, red, white etc. in the same plant. The skin is smooth and fragile, and the colour changes from green to red to dark purple as it matures. Mulberry is a common ingredient in many skin care creams due to its antioxidant powers include improving circulation, cardiovascular health and renal health. Eating mulberries regularly can also prevent cancer because of a phytoalexin called resveratrol.

Person Whom May Consume Muleberry

Parkinson Disease

Neurological diseases called Parkinson disease are associated with gamma-aminobutyric acid (GABA) cause to depletion in brain. Antioxidant activity present in White mulberry leaves is GABA-enriched, which may provide a neuroprotective effect against cerebral ischemia as well as neurotoxins. White mulberry leaf extracts contain antidopaminergic activity mediated through dopamine D2 receptors as documented by:

(a) Reducing haloperidol and metoclopramide-induced catalepsy in mice.

(b) Blocking amphetamine-induced stereotyped behaviour (such as schizophrenia) (c) And increasing the sensitivity to barbiturates.

Obesity

White mulberry regulates lipid metabolism, body weight gain, and adipose tissue by changing the expression of hepatic target genes in high-fat, diet-induced, obese mice. Melanin-concentrating hormone (MCH) is involved in feeding and energy metabolism. White mulberry leaf extract exhibits an antagonistic effect to MCH1 receptor in diet-induced obese mice, resulting in decreased body weight and adiposity, food intake, and hepatic lipid accumulation.

Gout

Morin extracted from white mulberry, at 80 mg/kg, exhibits hypouricemic action and inhibits xanthine oxidase in oxonate-induced hyperuricemic rats. The activity on urate uptake in rat renal brush border membrane vesicles was more potent than that of the prescription agent probenecid. Morin exhibits similar activity on urate transport in the human kidney.

Parasitic Infections

The leaves and roots of Mulberry can suppress the growth of infections caused by parasites. The use of gooseberry can be traced to traditional folk medicines.

Kidney Stones

There are four types of kidney stones. The most common type of stone is the calcium oxalate stone. These stones can be prevented by daily consumption of mulberry juice. Uric acid stones are often found in people with gout, but they may also occur in those who are dehydrated or who eat a high-protein diet. Struvite stones are connected with urinary tract infections. They can grow quickly and become large. Cysteine stones are the least common, and result from a hereditary disorder that causes the kidneys to excrete excessive amounts of some amino acids. Mulberries are added to medicines to strengthen the kidneys.

Blood Tonic

In Chinese medicine, a mulberry is considered as blood tonic, as they cleanse the blood and increase its production and strengthens the entire system.

Liver and Lung

In Chinese medicine, mulberry leaf tea is known as a cooling remedy that treats the liver and lung meridians. It removes lung heat symptoms such as fever, sore throat and cough, and it clears fire in the liver, that mean it removes symptoms such as dry, painful and watery eyes.

Pain

Extracts from Mulberry roots have sedative effects. It has found that it has analgesic and sedative component damnacanthal. It is recommended to treat menstrual cramps and other pains. Mulberry fruit juices were found to increase joint health and mobility. The juice can also help to prevent bone problems like arthritis and other skeletal disorders. Mulberry has xeronine and KB-C ingredients which aid in minimizing pain and swelling, relieving inflammatory conditions, and fortifying weak bones and ligaments.

Person Whom May Not Consume Mulberry

Chemotherapy Interference

A substance from mulberry root bark extract identified as albanol triggers cell death in human leukemia cells. It also suggests that mulberry extracts should not be used by anyone undergoing chemotherapy without the approval and supervision of a physician..

Skin Cancer

Mulberry extract is incorporated into skin-whitening products. The compound attributed with lightening the skin is arbutin, a form of hydroquinone that inhibits melanin release by suppressing the tyrosinase enzyme. A team of French researchers analyzed two cases of squamous cell carcinoma in women who had been using skin-lightening products for more than a decade. While they could not say for certain that hydroquinone agents were the direct cause of either cancer, they did note that the carcinogenic side effects of hydroquinone are well established in animal models.

Diabetes

White mulberry might lower the blood sugar levels in people for those who suffer from diabetes. Watch out the signs of low blood sugar (hypoglycemia) carefully if you have diabetes and use white mulberry.

Pregnancy/Lactation

Avoid use during pregnancy and lactation due to lack of clinical data.

CHAPTER 14

Orange, Olive

Orange

An orange—specifically, the sweet orange—is the citrus *Citrus* (*Citrus sinensis* (L.) Osbeck) fruit. It is the most commonly grown tree fruit in the world.

The orange is a hybrid of ancient cultivated origin, possibly between pomelo (*Citrus maxima*) and mandarin (*Citrus reticulata*). It is an evergreen flowering tree generally growing to 9-10 m in height (although very old specimens have reached 15 m). The leaves are arranged alternately, are ovate in shape with crenulate margins and are 4-10 cm long. The orange fruit is a hesperidium, a type of berry.

Orange trees are widely cultivated in tropical and subtropical climates for the sweet fruit, which is peeled or cut (to avoid the bitter rind) and eaten whole, or processed to extract orange juice, and also for the fragrant peel. In 2008, 68.5 million tons of oranges were grown worldwide, primarily in Brazil and the US states California and Florida.

Oranges probably originated in Southeast Asia and were cultivated in China by 2500 BC. The fruit of *Citrus sinensis* is called *sweet orange* to distinguish it from *Citrus aurantium*, the bitter orange. The name is thought to derive ultimately from the Sanskrit for the orange tree, with its final form developing after passing through numerous intermediate languages.

In a number of languages, it is known as a "Chinese apple", e.g., Dutch *sinaasappel* ("China's apple") or *appelsien*, or northern German *Apfelsine*. In English, however, "Chinese apple" generally refers to the pomegranate.

Oranges cannot be artificially ripened and must be mature when harvested. (In Texas, Arizona, California and Florida, laws forbid harvesting immature fruit for human consumption.) Ripe oranges, however, often have some green or yellow-green colour in the skin. Ethylene gas is used to turn green skin orange. The process is called "degreening", or sometimes, "gassing", "sweating" or "curing". Its purpose is to remove the green colour from otherwise mature fruit.

Degreening is used primarily in the early fall when night temperatures have not been low enough for the peel to develop its characteristic mature colour. Late oranges such as Valencia sometimes regreen during the spring growth flush and may also be degreened.

Recommended degreening conditions include 82 to 85 °F temperature, 92 to 95 per cent relative humidity and 1 to 5 ppm ethylene. Air circulation within the degreening room should produce about one change per minute. In addition, outside air ventilation should be adequate to maintain carbon dioxide level below one percent, which normally requires about one complete change of air per hour.

Degreening time varies with the amount of green colour, size of fruit and some cultural practices, e.g., excessive nitrogen fertilization promoting vigorous growth and oil-emulsion sprays after mid-July. Maximum degreening times in the US are 48 to 60 hours for oranges, but the degreening period should be as short as possible.

Products made from Oranges

Orange juice is one of the commodities traded on the New York Board of Trade. Brazil is the largest producer of orange juice in the world, followed by the USA. It is made by squeezing the fruit on a special instrument called a "*juicer*" or a "*squeezer*." The juice is collected in a small tray underneath. This is mainly done in the home, and in industry is done on a much larger scale.

Frozen orange juice concentrate is made from freshly squeezed and filtered orange juice.

Sweet orange oil is a by-product of the juice industry produced by pressing the peel. It is used as a flavouring of food and drink and for its fragrance in perfume and aromatherapy. Sweet orange oil consists of about 90 per cent d-limonene, a solvent used in various household chemicals, such as to condition wooden furniture, and along with other citrus oils in grease removal and as a hand-cleansing agent. It is an efficient cleaning agent which is promoted as being environmentally friendly and preferable to petroleum distillates.

However, d-Limonene is classified from slightly toxic to humans to very toxic to marine life in different countries. Its smell is considered more pleasant by some than those of other cleaning agents.

Although once thought to cause renal cancer in rats, limonene now is known as a chemopreventive agent with potential value as a dietary anti-cancer tool in humans. There is no evidence for carcinogenicity or genotoxicity in humans. The Carcinogenic Potency Project estimates that it causes human cancer on a level roughly equivalent to that caused by exposure to caffeic acid via dietary coffee intake. The IARC classifies *d*-limonene under Class 3: *not classifiable as to its carcinogenicity to humans*.

The orange blossom, which is the state flower of Florida, is highly fragrant and traditionally associated with good fortune. It has long been popular in bridal bouquets and head wreaths for weddings.

- Orange blossom essence is an important component in the making of perfume.
- The petals of orange blossom can also be made into a delicately citrus-scented version of rosewater; orange

blossom water (aka orange flower water) is a common part of both French and Middle Eastern cuisines, most often as an ingredient in desserts and baked goods.

- In the United States, orange flower water is used to make orange blossom scones and marshmallows.
- The orange blossom gives its touristic nickname to the *Costa del Azahar* ("Orange-blossom coast"), the Castellon seaboard.
- In Spain, fallen blossoms are dried and then used to make tea.
- Orange blossom honey, or actually citrus honey, is produced by putting beehives in the citrus groves during bloom, which also pollinates seeded citrus varieties. Orange blossom honey is highly prized, and tastes much like orange.
- Marmalade, a conserve usually made with Seville oranges. All parts of the orange are used to make marmalade: the pith and pips are separated, and typically placed in a muslin bag where they are boiled in the juice (and sliced peel) to extract their pectin, aiding the setting process.
- Orange peel is used by gardeners as a slug repellent.
- Orange leaves can be boiled to make tea.
- Orange wood sticks (also spelt orangewood) are used as cuticle pushers in manicures and pedicures, and as spudgers for manipulating slender electronic wires
- Orange wood is a flavouring wood in meat grilling much as mesquite, oak, pecan and hickory are used.

Olive

The olive is the fruit belongs to olive tree or "oliver". It is considered as the important food crop in Italy, Spain and especially in Greece among other countries around the Mediterranean. This fruit is naturally very bitter, but after a long time in salt, it becomes a tasty and healthy food. Olive oil is the juice made by crushing olives.

In Roman,the olive branches are used as a symbol of peace. In Christianity, too, it is seen as a symbol of peace, because according to the Bible, a dove brought an olive branch to Noah to show that the flood was over.

Person Whom May Consume Olive

. Cancer

The antioxidant and anti-inflammatory properties of olives make them for protection against cancer because chronic oxidative stress and chronic inflammation can be key factors in the development of cancer. If our cells get overwhelmed by oxidative stress and chronic inflammation, risk of cell cancer is increased. Olives can help us avoid this dangerous combination of chronic oxidative stress and chronic inflammation.

Breast cancer can be treated using triterpene phytonutrients in olives, including erythrodiol, uvaol and oleanolic acid. These olive phytonutrients have been shown to help interrupt the life cycle of breast cancer cells. Interruption of cell cycles has also been shown in the case of gastric cancer.

Antioxidant phytonutrients in olives may have a special ability to protect DNA (deoxyribonucleic acids) from oxygen damage. DNA protection from unwanted oxidative stress means better cell function in wide variety of ways and provides cells with decreased risk of cancer development.

Cardiovascular

One of the best ways to avoid oxidative stress is to consume a diet that is rich in antioxidant nutrients. The second of these circumstances is ongoing (chronic) and undesirable low-level inflammation. Undesirable and chronic inflammation can result from a variety of factors, including unbalanced metabolism, lifestyle, unwanted exposure to environmental contaminants, and other factors. One of the best ways to help avoid chronic and unwanted inflammation is to consume a diet that is rich in anti-inflammatory nutrients. Few foods are as rich in these compounds as extra virgin olive oil to cure cardiovascular system.

Digestion

Many of these anti-cancer effects in the digestive tract were believed to depend on the polyphenols in olive oil and their antioxidant plus anti-inflammatory properties continues to be a focus in research on prevention of digestive tract cancers. Numerous polyphenols in olive oil slows the growth of unwanted bacteria, including bacteria commonly responsible for digestive tract infections.

Bone Health

Bone health is a promising area of olive oil research. Better blood levels of calcium have been repeatedly associated with olive oil intake. Olive oil may eventually prove to have special bone benefits for post-menopausal women, who had been fed olive oil after having their ovaries.

Osteoporosis

A high consumption of olive oil appears to improve bone mineralization and calcification. It helps in calcium absorption and plays a vital role in aiding sufferers and in preventing the onset of Osteoporosis.

Stroke

Individuals who consume olive oil daily may be able to protect themselves from stroke.The "intensive" users of olive oil, those that used for both cooking and dressings had a 41 percent lower risk of stroke compared to those that did not use olive oil at all. By intake of this fruit provides much effective in reduction of stroke.

Rheumatoid Arthritis

People who had the lowest lifetime consumption of extra olive oil had two and a half times greater probability of developing rheumatoid arthritis than those with the highest lifetime consumption. If somebody suffers from rheumatoid arthritis, you must be familiar with the pain and inconvenience it can cause. Adding olive oil to your diet could help you protect yourself against rheumatoid arthritis.

Aging

Diets that are deficient in vitamin E accelerate the breakdown of certain fatty acids, leads to aging. The vitamin E content in olive oil is thought to provide a defence against such effects, and thus help to maintain mental faculties and muscular control longer and better. The vitamin A helps prevent and minimise the development of skin wrinkles.

CHAPTER 15

Passion Fruit, Papaya, Peaches, Pear, Persimmon, Pineapple, Plum, Pomegranate, Pomelo

Passion Fruit

Passiflora edulis is a vine species of passion flower that is native to Paraguay, Brazil and northern Argentina (Corrientes and Misiones provinces, among others). Its common names include passion fruit (UK and US), and passion fruit (Australia and New Zealand), purple granadilla and maracuja. In Colombia, the purple passion fruit is referred to as "gulupa", to distinguish it from the yellow maracuyá.

It is cultivated commercially in warmer, frost-free areas for its fruit and is widely grown in India, Sri Lanka, New Zealand, the Caribbean, Brazil, Colombia, Bolivia, Ecuador, Indonesia, Peru, Puerto Rico, Dominican Republic, California, Florida, Haiti, Hawaii, Argentina, Australia, East Africa, Mexico, Israel, Costa Rica, Venezuela, South Africa and Portugal.

The passion fruit is round to oval, either yellow or dark purple at maturity, with a soft to firm, juicy interior filled with numerous seeds. The fruit is both eaten and juiced; passion fruit juice is often added to other fruit juices to enhance the aroma.

The two types of passion fruit have clearly differing exterior appearances. The bright yellow variety of passion fruit, which is also known as the Golden Passion Fruit, can grow up to the size of a grapefruit, has a smooth, glossy, light and airy rind, and has been used as a rootstock for the Purple Passion Fruit in Australia. The dark purple passion fruit is smaller than a lemon, though it is less acidic than the yellow passion fruit, and has a richer aroma and flavour. It tastes like lemons, guava and pineapple combined.

The purple varieties of the fruit have been found to contain traces of cyanogenic glycosides in the skin.

- In Portugal, especially the Azores, passion fruit is used as a base for a variety of liqueurs.
- In Brazil, passion fruit mousse is a common dessert, and passion fruit seeds are routinely used to decorate the tops of cakes. Passion fruit juice is also very common. When making Caipirinha, it is common to use passion fruit instead of lime; it is then called "caipifruta de maracujá". It is also used as a mild sedative, and its active ingredient is commercialized under several brands, most notably Maracugina.
- In Colombia this is one of the most important fruits, especially for juices and desserts. It is a common fruit all over the country and there you can find 3 kinds of "Maracuyá" fruit.
- In the Dominican Republic, where it is locally called *chinola,* it is used to make juice and fruit preserves. Passion fruit-flavoured syrup is used on shaved ice, and the fruit is also eaten raw sprinkled with sugar.
- In Hawaii, passion fruit is locally called *lilikoi* and comes in yellow and purple varieties. Hawaiians eat the fruit raw, cracking the rind of the passion fruit either with their hands or teeth and sucking out the flavourful pulp and seeds. Passion fruit can also be cut in half and the seeds scooped out with a spoon. Lilikoi-flavoured syrup is a popular topping for shave ice. It is used as a desert flavoring for malasadas, cheesecakes, cookies, ice cream and mochi. Passion fruit is also favoured as a jam or jelly, as well as a butter. Most passion fruit comes from

backyard gardens or is wild-collected. While it can be found at farmers' markets throughout the islands, fruits are seldom sold in grocery stores.

- In Indonesia, there are two types of passionfruit (local name: 'markisa'), white flesh and yellow flesh. The white one is normally eaten straight as a fruit. The yellow one is commonly strained to obtain its juice, which is cooked with sugar to make thick syrup. Bottles or plastic jugs of concentrated syrup (generally produced in Sumatra from fruit grown in theLake Toba region) are sold in many supermarkets. Dilution of one part syrup to four (or more) parts water is recommended.
- In New Zealand and Australia, where it is called "passionfruit", it is available commercially both fresh and tinned. Fresh passionfruit is eaten for breakfast in the Summer months, is added to fruit salads, and fresh fruit pulp or passion fruit sauce is commonly used in desserts, including as a topping for pavlova (a regional meringue cake) and ice cream, a flavouring for cheesecake, and in the icing of vanilla slices. A passionfruit-flavoured soft drink called Passiona has also been manufactured in Australia for several decades.
- In Paraguay, passion fruit is used mainly to make juice, prepare desserts like passion fruit mousse, cheesecake, ice cream, to flavour yogurts and cocktails.
- In Mexico, passion fruit is used to make juice or is eaten raw with chilli powder and lime.
- In Puerto Rico, where the fruit is known as "Parcha", it is widely believed to lower blood pressure, probably because it contains harmala alkaloids and is a mild RIMA. Passion fruit juice is also very common there and is used in juices, ice cream or pastries.
- In Peru, passion fruit is used in several desserts, especially cheesecakes. It is also drunk alone as passion fruit juice and used in ceviche variations and in cocktails, including the passion fruit sour, a variation of the Pisco Sour.

- In the Philippines, passion fruit is commonly sold in public markets and in public schools. Some vendors sell the fruit with a straw in it to suck the seeds and juices inside. It is not very popular because of its sour flavour, and the fruit is very seasonal.
- In South Africa, passion fruit, known locally as Granadilla (the yellow variety as Guavadilla), is used to flavour yogurt. It is also used to flavour soft drinks such as Schweppes Sparkling Granadilla and numerous cordial drinks. It is often eaten raw or used as a topping for cakes and tarts. Granadilla juice is commonly available in restaurants. The yellow variety is used for juice processing, while the purple variety is sold in fresh fruit markets.
- In Sri Lanka passion fruit juice, along with faluda is one of the most popular refreshments. Passion fruit cordial is manufactured both at home as well as industrially by mixing the pulp with sugar, there being a large quantity of cordial manufacturers, suppliers and exporters in the country.
- In the United States, it is often used as an ingredient in juice mixes.
- In Vietnam, passion fruit is blended with honey and ice to create refreshing smoothies.
- In Thailand, passion fruit is called "Saowarot". The fruit is eaten whole and is also commonly juiced and drunk. Young shoots are cooked in curries or eaten with nam phrik

Nutritional Value per 100 g (3.5 oz)

Energy	406 kJ (97 kcal)
Carbohydrates	23.38 g
Sugars	11.20 g
Dietary fibre	10.4 g
Fat	0.70 g

Protein	2.20 g
Vitamin A equiv.	64 μg (8%)
Riboflavin (vit. B_2)	0.130 mg (11%)
Niacin (vit. B3)	1.500 mg (10%)
Folate (vit. B9)	14 μg (4%)
Vitamin C	30.0 mg (36%)
Calcium	12 mg (1%)
Iron	1.60 mg (12%)
Magnesium	29 mg (8%)
Phosphorus	68 mg (10%)
Potassium	348 mg (7%)
Zinc	0.10 mg (1%)

Fresh passion fruit is high in beta carotene, potassium, and dietary fibre. Passion fruit juice is a good source of ascorbic acid (vitamin C) , and good for people who have high blood pressure. Some research is showing that purple passion fruit peel may help with controlling asthma symptoms. The fruit contains Lycopene in the mature and immature pericarp.

Papaya

The papaya (from Carib via Spanish), papaw, or pawpaw is the fruit of the plant *Carica papaya*, the sole species in the genus *Carica* of the plant family Caricaceae. It is native to the tropics of the Americas, and was first cultivated in Mexico several centuries before the emergence of the Mesoamerican classical civilizations.

The papaya is a large tree-like plant, with a single stem growing from 5 to 10 metres (16 to 33 ft) tall, with spirally arranged leaves confined to the top of the trunk. The lower trunk is conspicuously scarred where leaves and fruit were borne. The leaves are large, 50-70 centimetres (20-28 in) diametre, deeply palmately lobed with 7 lobes. The tree is usually unbranched, unless lopped. The flowers are similar in shape to the flowers of the *Plumeria*, but are much smaller and wax-like. They appear on the axils of the leaves, maturing into the large 15-45 centimetres (5.9-18 in) long, 10-30 centimetres (3.9-12 in) diametre fruit. The fruit is ripe when it feels soft (as soft as a ripe avocado or a bit softer) and its skin has attained an amber to orange hue.

Two kinds of papayas are commonly grown. One has sweet, red (or orangish) flesh, and the other has yellow flesh; in Australia these are called "red papaya" and "yellow papaw", respectively. Either kind, picked green, is called a "green papaya."

The large-fruited, red-fleshed 'Maradol', 'Sunrise', and 'Caribbean Red' papayas often sold in U.S. markets are commonly grown in Mexico and Belize.

'SunUp' and 'Rainbow' are genetically modified cultivars developed in Hawaii that are resistant to the papaya ringspot virus.

Papayas can be used as a food, a cooking aid, and in traditional medicine. The stem and bark may be used in rope production.

Papaya fruit is a rich source of nutrients such as provitamin A carotenoids, vitamin C, B vitamins, dietary minerals and dietary fibre. Papaya skin, pulp and seeds also contain a variety of phytochemicals, including natural phenols. Danielone is a phytoalexin found in the papaya fruit. This compound showed high antifungal activity against *Colletotrichum gloesporioides*, a pathogenic fungus of papaya.

The ripe fruit of the papaya is usually eaten raw, with or without skin or seeds.

The unripe green fruit can be eaten cooked, usually in curries, salads, and stews. Green papaya is used in Southeast Asian cooking, both raw and cooked. In Thai cuisine, papaya is used to make *som tam* and *kaeng som* when still not fully ripe. In Indonesian cuisine, the unripe green fruits and young leaves are boiled for use as part of lalab salad, while the flower buds are sautéed and stir fried with chillies and green tomatoes as Minahasan papaya flower vegetable dish. Papayas have a relatively high amount of pectin, which can be used to make jellies. The smell of ripe, fresh papaya flesh can strike some people as unpleasant.

The black seeds of the papaya are edible and have a sharp, spicy taste. They are sometimes ground and used as a substitute for black pepper.

In some parts of Asia, the young leaves of the papaya are steamed and eaten like spinach.

In some parts of the world, papaya leaves are made into tea as a treatment for malaria. Anti-malarial and anti-plasmodial activity has been noted in some preparations of the plant, but the mechanism is not understood and no treatment method based on these results has been scientifically proven.

Papaya is frequently used as a hair conditioner, but should be used in small amounts. Papaya releases a latex fluid when not quite ripe, which can cause irritation and provoke allergic reaction in some people. The papaya fruit, seeds, latex, and leaves also contains carpaine, an anthelmintic alkaloid (a drug that removes parasitic worms from the body), which can be dangerous in high doses.

It is speculated that the latex concentration of unripe papayas may cause uterine contractions, which may lead to a miscarriage. Papaya seed extracts in large doses have a contraceptive effect on rats and monkeys, but in small doses have no effect on the unborn animals.

Excessive consumption of papaya can cause carotenemia, the yellowing of soles and palms, which is otherwise harmless. However, a very large dose would need to be consumed; papaya contains about 6 per cent of the level of beta carotene found in carrots (the most common cause of carotenemia).

Person Whom May Consume Papaya

Protection Against Heart Disease

Papayas are very helpful for the prevention of atherosclerosis and diabetic heart disease. Papayas are an excellent source of vitamin C as well as a good source of vitamin E and vitamin A. These nutrients help prevent the oxidation of cholesterol. Only when cholesterol becomes oxidized, it able to stick to and build up in blood vessel walls, forming dangerous plaques that can cause heart attacks or strokes. One way in which dietary vitamin E and vitamin C may exert this effect is through their association with a compound called paraoxonase, an enzyme that inhibits LDL cholesterol and HDL cholesterol oxidation.

Papayas are good source of fibre, to lower high cholesterol levels. The folic acid found in papayas is needed for the conversion of a substance called homocysteine into amino acids such as cysteine or methionine. If unconverted, homocysteine can directly damage blood vessel walls, is considered a significant risk factor for a heart attack or stroke.

Colon Cancer

The nutrients in papaya has been helpful in the prevention of colon cancer. Its fibre is able to bind cancer-causing toxins in the colon and keep them away from the healthy colon cells. These nutrients provide synergistic protection for colon cells from free radical damage to their DNA. Increasing your intake of these papaya is good idea for individuals at risk of colon cancer.

Anti-Inflammatory Effects

Papaya contains several unique protein enzymes including papain and chymopapain. These enzymes help lower inflammation and to improve healing from burns. In addition, the antioxidant nutrients found in papaya, including vitamin C, vitamin E, and beta-carotene, are also good at reducing inflammation. This may explain why people with diseases that are worsened by inflammation, such as asthma, osteoarthritis, and rheumatoid arthritis, find that the severity of their condition is reduced when they get more of these nutrients.

Immune Support

Vitamin C and vitamin A, present in papaya made in the body from the beta-carotene are needed for the proper function of a healthy immune system. Papaya may therefore be a healthy for preventing such illnesses as recurrent ear infections, colds and flu.

Rheumatoid Arthritis

High doses of vitamin C makes osteoarthritis, a type of degenerative arthritis that occurs with aging, another indicates that vitamin C-rich foods, such as papaya, provide humans with protection against inflammatory polyarthritis, a form of rheumatoid arthritis involving two or more joints.

Promote Lung Health

If you are smoker, or if you are frequently exposed to secondhand smoke, then making vitamin A rich foods, such as papaya, your healthy way of eating save your life .vitamin A's protective effects may help explain why some smokers do not develop emphysema. "There are a lot of people who live to be 90 years old and are smokers" Why? Probably because of their diet. The implications are those who start smoking at an early age are more likely to become vitamin A deficient and develop complications associated with cancer and emphysema. If someone you love smokes, or if your work necessitates exposure to second hand smoke, protect yourself by making sure that at least one of the World's Healthiest Foods that are rich in vitamin A, such as papaya, is a daily part of your healthy way of eating.

Prevent Prostate Cancer

Eating regularly lycopene-rich fruits, such as papaya, may greatly reduce a man's risk of developing prostate cancer. In this case-control involving 130 prostate cancer patients and 274 hospital controls, men taking papaya were found to have an 86 per cent reduced risk of prostate cancer.

It was found between the men's consumption of lycopene-rich fruits and vegetables such as tomatoes, apricots, pink grapefruit, watermelon, papaya, and guava. Men who most frequently enjoyed these foods were 82 per cent less likely to have prostate cancer compared to those consuming the least lycopene-rich foods.

Regular consumption of foods which is rich in lycopene resulted in a synergistic protective effect, stronger than the protection afforded by either.

Digestive Process

If you have digestive problems, you must consume eating papayas. because they contain an enzyme called papain, which helps with the digestive process. It can prevent you from constipated and may also help end diarrhea. papain has also been used as a way to treat stings from bees and jellyfish. If there is nothing besides papaya available in the house, it may provide you with relief.

Relieve Nausea

If you often have nausea, it is because you have morning sickness or you get sick when you are traveling, you may want to consider adding papaya to your diet. Papaya is known to prevent this type of nausea or provide you with relief once you already have it.

Lung Protection

The papaya provides the body with lung protection is because it contains Vitamin A. When a person experiences lung cancer or other lung conditions, they often have a deficiency of Vitamin A. If you are worried about getting lung cancer due to secondhand smoke or working conditions, then you really may want to consider adding papaya to your daily diet.There are many people who believe that papaya will also help protect the heart from disease and the body from developing various forms of cancer.

Cure Dengue Fever

- The juice from papaya leaves can cure dengue fever.
- Wash the leaf and cut into smaller pieces.
- Squeeze the pulp and filter with the cloth.
- Two tablespoons serving per day.

It has a very bitter taste.hence it may provide some relief to dengue fever.

Skin Treatment

The papain is very useful for the treatment of various skin irritations and wounds. It has also been used for the treatment of bedsores, burns, wounds from surgical procedures and skin ulcers. Papain lotions are used on wounds in the healing process and not on open sores. When applied to the skin, be careful as not to let the ointment come in direct contact with open wounds.

Peaches

The fruit has yellow or whitish flesh, a delicate aroma, and a skin that is either velvety (peaches) or smooth (nectarines) in different cultivars. The flesh is very delicate and easily bruised in some cultivars, but is fairly firm in some commercial varieties, especially when green. The single, large seed is red-brown, oval shaped, approximately 1.3-2 cm long, and is surrounded by a wood-like husk. Peaches, along with cherries, plums and apricots, are stone fruits (drupes).

The scientific name *persica*, along with the word "peach" itself and its cognates in many European languages, derives from an early European belief that peaches were native to Persia (now Iran). The modern botanical consensus is that they originate in China, and were introduced to Persia and the Mediterranean region along the Silk Road before Christian times. The botanical name is derived from the Greek word for the fruit after it was introduced into the Mediterranean through Persia and from China.

Cultivated peaches are divided into clingstones and freestones, depending on whether the flesh sticks to the stone or not; both can have either white or yellow flesh. Peaches with white flesh typically are very sweet with little acidity, while yellow-fleshed peaches typically have an acidic tang coupled with sweetness, though this also varies greatly. Both colours often have some red on their skin. Low-acid white-fleshed peaches are the most popular kinds in China, Japan, and neighbouring Asian countries, while Europeans and North Americans have historically favoured the acidic, yellow-fleshed kinds.

Peaches should be stored at room temperature and refrigeration should be avoided as this can lessen the taste of the peach. Peaches are climacteric and hence they will continue ripening after being picked from the tree.

Health Benefits of Peaches

- Wonderfully delicious peaches are low in calories (100 g just provide 39 calories) and contain no saturated fats. Nonetheless, they are packed with numerous health promoting compounds, minerals and vitamins.
- The total measured anti-oxidant strength (ORAC value) of 100 g peach fruit is 1814 TE (Trolex equivalents).
- Fresh peaches are a moderate source of antioxidant, *vitamin* C. Vitamin-C has anti-oxidant effects and is required for connective tissue synthesis in the body. Consumption of foods rich in vitamin C helps the body develop resistance against infectious agents, and help scavenges harmful free radicals.
- Fresh fruits are an also moderate source of vitamin A and ß-carotene. ß-carotene is a pro-vitamin, which converts into vitamin A in the body. Vitamin A is essential for vision. It is also required for maintaining healthy mucus membranes and skin. Consumption of natural fruits rich in vitamin A is known to offer protection from lung and oral cavity cancers.
- They are rich in many vital minerals such as potassium, fluoride and iron. Iron is required for red blood cell formation. Fluoride is a component of bones and teeth and is essential for prevention of dental caries. Potassium is an important component of cell and body fluids that help regulate heart rate and blood pressure.
- Peaches contain health promoting flavonoid poly phenolic antioxidants such as *lutein, zea-xanthin* and *ß-cryptoxanthin.* These compounds help act as protective scavengers against oxygen-derived free radicals and reactive oxygen species (ROS) that play a role in aging and various disease processes.

Peaches have also been found to be beneficial for individuals suffering from the following ailments:

- Acidosis
- Anemia
- Asthma
- Bladder and Kidney Stones
- Bronchitis
- Constipation
- Dry Cough
- Gastritis
- High Blood Pressure
- Nephritis
- Poor Digestion

Pear

The pear is any of several tree species of genus *Pyrus* and also the name of the pomaceous fruit of these trees. Several species of pear are valued by humans for their edible fruit, but the fruit of other species is small, hard, and astringent.

The genus *Pyrus* is classified in subtribe Pyrinae within tribe Pyreae. The apple (*Malus domestica*), which it resembles in floral structure, is also a member of this subcategory.

The English word "pear" is probably from Common West Germanic *pera*, probably a loanword of Vulgar Latin *pira*, the plural of *pirum*, akin to Greek *apios* (from Mycenaean *ápisos*), which is likely of Semitic origin. The place name *Perry* and *Pharisoulopol* can indicate the historical presence of pear trees. The term "pyriform" is sometimes used to describe something which is "pear-shaped".

The fruit is composed of the receptacle or upper end of the flower-stalk (the so-called calyx tube) greatly dilated. Enclosed within its cellular flesh is the true fruit: five cartilaginous carpels, known colloquially as the "core". From the upper rim of the receptacle are given off the five sepals, the five petals, and the very numerous stamens.

The pear is very similar to the apple in cultivation, propagation and pollination. The pear and the apple are also related to the quince: all three fruits are members of the taxonomic subtribe Malinae.

Pears and apples cannot always be distinguished by the form of the fruit; some pears look very much like some apples. One major difference is that the flesh of pear fruit contains stone cells (also called "grit"). Pear trees and apple trees do have several visible differences.

According to Pear Bureau Northwest, about 3000 known varieties of pears are grown worldwide. In the United States, only 10 heirloom varieties are widely recognized: Green Bartlett, Red Bartlett, Bosc, Green Anjou, Red Anjou, Comice, Forelle, Seckel, Concorde, and Starkrimson.

Pears are consumed fresh, canned, as juice, and dried. The juice can also be used in jellies and jams, usually in combination with other fruits or berries. Fermented pear juice is called perry or pear cider.

Pears ripen at room temperature. They will ripen faster if placed next to bananas in a fruit bowl. Refrigeration will slow further ripening. Pear Bureau Northwest offers tips on ripening and judging ripeness: Although the skin on Bartlett pears changes from green to yellow as they ripen, most varieties show little colour change as they ripen. Because pears ripen from the inside out, the best way to judge ripeness is to "Check the Neck." To Check the Neck for ripeness, apply gentle thumb pressure to the neck, or stem end of the pear. If it yields to gentle pressure, then the pear is ripe, sweet, and juicy. If it is firm, leave pear at room temperature and Check the Neck daily for ripeness.

The culinary or cooking pear is green but dry and hard and only edible after several hours of cooking. Two Dutch cultivars are "Gieser Wildeman" and "Saint Remy". They are traditionally stewed in wine with spices and served both warm and cold.

Pear wood is one of the preferred materials in the manufacture of high-quality woodwind instruments and furniture. It is also used for wood carving, and as a firewood to produce aromatic smoke for smoking meat or tobacco. Pear wood is valued for kitchen spoons, scoops and stirrers, as it does not contaminate food with colour, flavor or smell and resists warping and splintering despite repeated soaking and drying cycles. Lincoln describes it as "a fairly tough, very stable wood (used for) carving brushbacks, umbrella handles, measuring instruments such as set squares and T-squares . . . recorders . . . violin and guitar fingerboards and piano keys... decorative veneering." Pearwood is the favoured wood for architect's rulers because it does not warp. It is similar to the wood of its relative, the apple tree, (*Pyrus malus* [also called *Malus domestica*]) and used for many of the same purposes.

Pear leaves were smoked in Europe before tobacco was introduced.

Health Benefits

Pear, Raw

Nutritional Value per 100 g (3.5 oz)	
Energy	242 kJ (58 kcal)
Carbohydrates	15.46 g
Sugars	9.80 g
Dietary fibre	3.1 g
Fat	0 g
Protein	0.38 g
Thiamine (vit. B_1)	0.012 mg (1%)
Riboflavin (vit. B_2)	0.025 mg (2%)
Niacin (vit. B_3)	0.157 mg (1%)
Pantothenic acid (B_5)	0.048 mg (1%)
Vitamin B_6	0.028 mg (2%)
Folate (vit. B_9)	7 µg (2%)

Vitamin C	4.2 mg (5%)
Calcium	9 mg (1%)
Iron	0.17 mg (1%)
Magnesium	7 mg (2%)
Phosphorus	11 mg (2%)
Potassium	119 mg (3%)
Zinc	0.10 mg (1%)

Pears are a good source of dietary fibre and a good source of vitamin C. Most of the vitamin C, as well as the dietary fibre, is contained within the skin of the fruit. According to the FDA's final rule dated July 25, 2006 "Food Labeling; Guidelines for Voluntary Nutrition Labeling of Raw Fruits, Vegetables, and Fish," the nutritional content of a medium-sized fresh pear weighing 166g/5.9oz is as follows:

Calories	100
Sodium	0 mg/0%
Potassium	190 mg/5%
Total carbohydrate	26 mg/9%
Dietary Fibre	6g/24%
Sugars	16g
Protein	1g
Vitamin C	10%
Calcium	2%

Pears are less allergenic than many other fruits, and pear juice is therefore sometimes used as the first juice introduced to infants. However, caution is recommended for all fruit juice consumption by infants, as studies have suggested a link between excessive fruit juice consumption and reduced nutrient intake, as well as a tendency towards obesity. Pears are low in salicylates and benzoates, so are recommended in exclusion diets for allergy sufferers. Along with lamb and rice, pears may form part of the strictest exclusion diet for allergy sufferers.

Most of the fibre is insoluble, making pears a good laxative. The gritty fibre content may reduce the number of cancerous colon polyps.

Person Whom May Consume Pear

Cardiovascular and Colonhealth

Pear had fibres which not only help you to avoid the hassles of constipation and regular bowel movements; it also helps to bind the bile salts in the colon and efficiently flushes them out of your system. Fibre lowers the cholesterol levels, tor those people suffering from atherosclerosis or diabetic heart disease. Since bile salts are made from cholesterol, the body must break down more cholesterol to make more bile, a substance that is also necessary for digestion. Eat the pear whole for its precious fibre that is highly beneficial for your colon health.

Fibre also binds the chemicals in the colon the reason for causing cancer, prevents them from damaging colon cells. This may be one reason why diets high in fibre-rich foods, such as pears, are associated with a reduced risk of colon cancer.

Post-menopausal Breast Cancer

Pears are rich in fibre. Consuming large amount of fibre, especially cereal fibre such as pears, reduce the risk of breast cancer. Women who have taken hormone replacement and have consumed lots of fibres have significantly lowered their risk of breast cancer by 50 per cent.

Macular Degeneration

Carrots would keep your eyes bright as a child, but as an adult, it looks like fruit is even more important for keeping your sight. Achieves of Ophthalmology indicates ,eating 3 or more servings of fruit per day may lower your risk of age-related macular degeneration (ARMD), the primary cause of vision loss in older adults, by 36 per cent, compared to persons who consume less than 1.5 servings of fruit daily.

The antioxidant vitamins A, C, and E and carotenoids on the development of early ARMD or neovascular ARMD, a more severe form of illness associated with vision loss. While, surprisingly, intake of vegetables, antioxidant, vitamins and carotenoids were not strongly related to incidence of either form of ARM, fruit intake was definitely protective against the severe form of this vision-destroying disease. Three servings of fruit may sound like a lot to eat each day, but pears can help you reach this goal. Add sliced pears to your morning cereal, lunch time yogurt.

Cancer

Pears contain good source of hydroxycinnamic acid, which has been identified as helping to prevent stomach cancer. The high vitamin C and copper content act as good anti-oxidants that protect cells from damages by free radicals. At least one serving of pears a day is associated with a reduced risk of lung cancer in women. The high vitamin C and copper content act as good antioxidants that protect cells from damage by free radicals.

Constipation

Pectin present in pears is diuretic and thus may have mild laxative effect. Consuming pear juice regularly helps to regulate bowel movements. A high sorbitol content plus extra fibre makes pears ideal for persons those who suffer by constipation.

Shortness of Breath

Due to summer heat children might have shortness of breath with excessive phlegm. Drink pear juice during this period to help clear the phlegm.

Persimmon

A persimmon is the edible fruit of a number of species of trees in the genus *Diospyros* in the ebony wood family (Ebenaceae). The word *Diospyros* means "the fire of Zeus" in ancient Greek. As a tree, it is a perennial plant. The word *persimmon* is derived from *putchamin, pasiminan*, or *pessamin*, from Powhatan, an Algonquian language of the eastern United States, meaning "a dry fruit". Persimmons are generally light yellow-orange to dark red-orange in colour, and depending on the species, vary in size from 1.5 to 9 cm (0.5 to 4 in) in diameter, and may be spherical, acorn-, or pumpkin-shaped. The calyx often remains attached to the fruit after harvesting, but becomes easier to remove as it ripens. They are high in glucose, with a balanced protein profile, and possess various medicinal and chemical uses.

Commercially, there are generally two types of persimmon fruit: astringent and non-astringent.

The heart-shaped Hachiya is the most common variety of astringent persimmon. Astringent persimmons contain very high levels of soluble tannins and are unpalatably astringent (or "furry" tasting) if eaten before softening. The astringency of tannins is removed through ripening by exposure to light over several days, wrapping the fruit in paper (probably because this increases the ethylene concentration of the surrounding air), and/or artificially with chemicals such as alcohol and carbon dioxide which change tannin into the insoluble form. This bletting process is sometimes jumpstarted by exposing the fruit to cold or frost which quickens cellular wall breakdown. These astringent persimmons can also be prepared for commercial purposes by drying. Tanenashi fruit will occasionally contain a seed or two, which can be planted and will yield a larger more vertical tree than when merely grafted onto the *D. virginiana* rootstock most commonly used in the U.S. Such seedling trees may produce fruit that bears more seeds, usually 6 to 8 per fruit, and the fruit itself may vary slightly from the parent tree. Seedlings are said to be more susceptible to root nematodes.

The non-astringent persimmon is squat like a tomato and is most commonly sold as *fuyu*. Non-astringent persimmons are not actually free of tannins as the term suggests, but rather are far less astringent before ripening, and lose more of their tannic quality sooner. Non-astringent persimmons may be consumed when still very firm, and remain edible when very soft.

There is a third type, less commonly available, the pollination-variant non-astringent persimmons. When fully pollinated, the flesh of these fruit is brown inside – known as *goma* in Japan – and the fruit can be eaten firm. These varieties are highly sought after and can be found at specialty markets or farmers markets only. Tsurunoko, sold as "Chocolate persimmon" for its dark brown flesh, Maru, sold as "Cinnamon persimmon" for its spicy flavor, and Hyakume, sold as "Brown sugar" are the three best known.

Before ripening, persimmons usually have a "chalky" taste or bitter taste. Persimmons are eaten fresh, dried, raw, or cooked. When eaten fresh they are usually eaten whole like an apple or cut into quarters, though with some varieties it is best to peel the skin first. One way to consume very ripe persimmons, which can have the texture of pudding, is to remove the top leaf with a paring knife and scoop out the flesh with a spoon. Riper persimmons can also be eaten by removing the top leaf, breaking the fruit in half and eating from the inside out. The flesh ranges from firm to mushy, and the texture is unique. The flesh is very sweet and when firm due to being unripe, possesses an apple-like crunch.

The Sharon fruit was found to contain high levels of dietary fibre, phenolic compounds, potassium, magnesium, calcium, iron and manganese. They are also rich in vitamin C and beta carotene. Regular consumption of the fruit is believed to reduce the risk of atherosclerosis heart attacks. A separate research project showed that a diet rich in Sharon fruit persimmons improved lipid metabolism – the way the body copes with fat – in laboratory rats.

The fruits of some persimmon varieties contain the tannins catechin and gallocatechin, as well as the candidate anti-tumor compounds betulinic acid and shibuol.

It is used as a fixed Chinese remedy for hiccups. Its good for staying Young and healthy.

Persimmon cake is also used as a conventional medicine for diarrhea, hemorrhoids, lung infections and asthma. To make persimmon cake the fruit must be plucked when the skin starts turning yellow in colour.

Astringent taste of persimmon can help stop diarrhea, reduces sweating, and slows or stops bleeding.

- Persimmons can help to prevent cancer due to high content of vitamin A.
- Persimmon is good for skin. It makes for an excellent facial mask.
- Persimmon fruits contain healthy amounts of minerals like potassium, manganese, copper and phosphorus. These are believed to be powerful free radical scavengers and boost the production of blood cells.

Pineapple

Pineapple (*Ananas comosus*), a tropical plant with edible multiple fruit consisting of coalesced berries, named for resemblance to the pine cone, is the most economically important plant in the *Bromeliaceae* family. Pineapples may be cultivated from a crown cutting of the fruit, possibly flowering in 20-24 months and fruiting in the following six months.

Pineapple may be consumed fresh, canned, juiced, and are found in a wide array of food stuffs - dessert, fruit salad, jam, yogurt, ice cream, candy, and as a complement to meat dishes. In addition to consumption, in the Philippines the pineapple's leaves are used as the source of a textile fibre called piña, and is employed as a component of wall paper and furnishings, amongst other uses.

The pineapple is a herbaceous perennial which grows to 1.0 to 1.5 meters (3.3 to 4.9 ft) tall, although sometimes it can be taller. In appearance, the plant itself has a short, stocky stem with tough, waxy leaves. When creating its fruit, it usually produces up to 200 flowers, although some large-fruited cultivars can exceed this. Once it flowers, the individual fruits of the flowers join together to create what is commonly referred to as a pineapple. After the first fruit is produced, side shoots (called 'suckers' by commercial growers) are produced in the leaf axils of the main stem. These may be removed for propagation, or left to produce additional fruits on the original plant. Commercially, suckers that appear around the base are cultivated. It has 30 or more long, narrow, fleshy, trough-shaped leaves with sharp spines along the margins that are 30 to 100 centimeters (1.0 to 3.3 ft) long, surrounding a thick stem. In the first year of growth, the axis lengthens and thickens, bearing numerous leaves in close spirals. After 12 to 20 months, the stem grows into a spike-like inflorescence up to 15 cm (6 in) long with over 100 spirally arranged, trimerous flowers, each subtended by a bract. Flower colours vary, depending on variety, from lavender, through light purple to red.

The ovaries develop into berries which coalesce into a large, compact, multiple accessory fruit. The fruit of a pineapple is arranged in two interlocking helices, eight in one direction, thirteen in the other, each being a Fibonacci number.

Pineapple carries out CAM photosynthesis, fixing carbon dioxide at night and storing it as the acid malate and then releasing it during the day, aiding photosynthesis.

Raw pineapple is an excellent source of manganese (45% DV in a 100 g serving) and vitamin C (80% DV per 100 g).

Mainly from its stem, pineapple contains a proteolytic enzyme, bromelain, which breaks down protein. If having sufficient bromelain content raw pineapple juice can thus be used as a marinade and tenderizer for meat. Pineapple enzymes can interfere with the preparation of some foods, such as jelly or other gelatin-based desserts, but would be destroyed during cooking and the canning process. The quantity of bromelain in the fruit is probably not significant, being mostly in the inedible stalk. Furthermore, an ingested enzyme like bromelain is unlikely to survive intact the proteolytic processes of digestion.

Some buyers prefer green fruit, others ripened or off-green. A plant growth regulator, Ethephon, is typically sprayed onto the fruit one week before harvest, developing ethylene, which turns the fruit golden yellow. After cleaning and slicing, they are typically canned in sugar syrup with added preservative.

A pineapple will never become any riper than it was when harvested, though a fully ripe pineapple can bruise and rot quickly.

The fruit itself is quite perishable and storage of it should be taken seriously. If it is stored at room temperature, it should be used within two days; however, if it is refrigerated, the time span is extended to five to seven days.

The flesh and juice of pineapples are used in cuisines around the world. In many tropical countries, pineapple is prepared, and sold on roadsides as a snack. They are sold whole, or in halves with a stick inserted. Whole, cored slices with a cherry in the middle are a common garnish on hams in the West. Chunks of pineapple are not only used in desserts such as fruit salad, but also as a main ingredient in savory dishes, such in hamburgers, and as a pizza topping. Crushed pineapple is used in yogurt, jam, sweets, and ice cream. The juice of the pineapple is served as a beverage, and is also as a main ingredient in such cocktails as the Piña colada.

Person Whom May Consume Pineapple

Macular Degeration

Macular degeneration is an age related medical condition which affects vision. This leads to loss of vision in the midpoint of the visual field due to damage to the retina. However, eating pineapple degreases your chances by 36 per cent. You can feel safe from this horrible disease. You can add these to your morning cereal or lunch time yogurt.

Bone Strength

The benefits of pineapples are popular due to their ability to build and maintain strong bones. Pineapples are rich in manganese, a trace mineral that is needed for your body to build bone and connective tissues. In fact, if you consume a cup of pineapple, you can already get 73 percent of your total body requirement for manganese.

Gums Healthy

Gums are very important to keep healthy .If a person has unhealthy gums, his/her teeth would be in bad condition, and eventually will fall out. Eating pineapple will strengthen your gums that will help keep your teeth healthy and strong.

Arthritis

Eating pineapples can greatly alleviate the pain of arthritis while at the same time improve the condition by strengthening the bones. When you eat pineapples, you have a better chance at having a healthier life.

Hypertension

Hypertension occurs when too much force given on the artery walls while the blood circulates. One of the best ways to combat this is to take high amount of potassium plus a small amount of sodium in your diet. Pineapples are the correct for hypertension, since a cup of pineapple contains about 1 mg of sodium and 195 mg of potassium.

Lose Weight

Eating pineapple can highly cut down your sweet cravings because of its natural sweetness, saving you from a lot of sugar-induced calories. Consuming a lot of pineapple in your meals will leads to weight loss because pineapples can make you feel full without giving you an ounce of fat.

Plum

A plum or gage is a stone fruit tree in the genus *Prunus*, subgenus *Prunus*. The subgenus is distinguished from other subgenera (peaches, cherries, bird cherries, etc.) in the shoots having a terminal bud and solitary side buds (not clustered), the flowers in groups of one to five together on short stems, and the fruit having a groove running down one side and a smooth stone (or *pit*).

Mature plum fruit may have a dusty-white coating that gives them a glaucous appearance; this is easily rubbed off. This is an epicuticular wax coating and is known as "wax bloom". Dried plum fruits are called dried plums or prunes, although prunes are a distinct type of plum, and may have antedated the fruits now commonly known as plums.

Plum fruit tastes sweet and/or tart; the skin may be particularly tart. It is juicy and can be eaten fresh or used in jam-making or other recipes. Plum juice can be fermented into plum wine; when distilled, this produces a brandy known in Eastern Europe as *Slivovitz*, *Rakia*, *Tuica* or *Pálinka*. In central England, a cider-like alcoholic beverage known as plum jerkum is made from plums.

Dried plums (or prunes) are also sweet and juicy and contain several antioxidants. Plums and prunes are known for their laxative effect. This effect has been attributed to various compounds present in the fruits, such as dietary fibre, sorbitol, and isatin. Prunes and prune juice are often used to help regulate the functioning of the digestive system. Dried prune marketers in the United States have, in recent years, begun marketing their product as "dried plums". This is due to "prune" having negative connotations connected with elderly people suffering from constipation.

Dried, salted plums are used as a snack, sometimes known as *saladito* or *salao*. Various flavors of dried plum are available at Chinese grocers and specialty stores worldwide. They tend to be much drier than the standard prune. Cream, ginsing, spicy, and salty are among the common varieties. Licorice is generally used to intensify the flavor of these plums and is used to make salty plum drinks and toppings for shaved ice or *baobing*.

Pickled plums are another type of preserve available in Asia and international specialty stores. The Japanese variety, called *umeboshi*, is often used for rice balls, called *onigiri* or *omusubi*. The *ume*, from which *umeboshi* are made, is more closely related, however, to the apricot than to the plum.

As with many other members of the rose family, plum seeds contain cyanogenic glycosides, including amygdalin. These substances are capable of decomposing into a sugar molecule and hydrogen cyanide gas. While plum seeds are not the most toxic within the rose family (the bitter almond is the most toxic , large doses of these chemicals from any source are hazardous to human health.

Prune kernel oil is made from the fleshy inner part of the pit of the plum.

Plums come in a wide variety of colours and sizes. Some are much firmer-fleshed than others, and some have yellow, white, green or red flesh, with equally varying skin colour.

Plum cultivars in use today include:

- Damson or Damask plum
- Greengage (firm, green flesh and skin even when ripe)
- Mirabelle (dark yellow, predominantly grown in northeast France)
- Satsuma plum (firm red flesh with a red skin)
- Victoria (yellow flesh with a red or mottled skin)
- Yellowgage or golden plum (similar to greengage, but yellow)

When it flowers in the early spring, a plum tree will be covered in blossoms, and in a good year approximately 50 per cent of the flowers will be pollinated and become plums. Flowering starts after 80 growing degree days.

If the weather is too dry, the plums will not develop past a certain stage, but will fall from the tree while still tiny, green buds, and if it is unseasonably wet or if the plums are not harvested as soon as they are ripe, the fruit may develop a fungal condition called brown rot. Brown rot is not toxic, and very small affected areas can be cut out of the fruit, but unless the rot is caught immediately, the fruit will no longer be edible. Plum is used as a food plant by the larvae of some Lepidoptera, including November moth, willow beauty and short-cloaked moth.

A large number of plums, of the Damson variety, are also grown in Hungary, where they are called *szilva* and are used to make *lekvar* (a plum paste jam), *palinka* (a *slivovitz*-type liquor), plum dumplings, and other foods. The region of Szabolcs-Szatmár, in the northeastern part of the country near the borders with Ukraine and Romania, is a major producer of plums.

The plum blossom or *meihua* , along with the peony, are considered traditional floral emblems of China.

The plum is commonly used in China, Yunnan area, to produce a local plum wine with a smooth, sweet, fruity taste and approximately 12 per cent alcohol by volume.

Pomegranate

The pomegranate , *Punica granatum*, is a fruit-bearing deciduous shrub or small tree growing between five and eight meters tall.

Native to the area of modern day Iran and Iraq, the pomegranate has been cultivated in the Caucasus since ancient times. From there it spread to Asian areas such as the Caucasus as well as the Himalayas in Northern India. Today, it is widely cultivated throughout Turkey, Iran, Syria, Azerbaijan, Armenia, Afghanistan, India, Pakistan, Bangladesh, Iraq, Lebanon, Egypt, China, Burma, Saudi Arabia, Israel, Jordan, the drier parts of southeast Asia, the Mediterranean region of Southern Europe, and tropical Africa. Introduced into Latin America and California by Spanish settlers in 1769, pomegranate is also cultivated in parts of California and Arizona for juice production.

In the Northern Hemisphere, the fruit is typically in season from September to February. In the Southern Hemisphere, the pomegranate is in season from March to May.

The pomegranate has been mentioned in many ancient texts, notably the Book of Exodus, the Homeric Hymns and the Quran. In recent years, it has reached mainstream prominence in the commercial markets of North America and the Western Hemisphere.

After opening the pomegranate by scoring it with a knife and breaking it open, the arils (seed casings) are separated from the peel and internal white pulp membranes. Separating the red arils is easier in a bowl of water, because the arils sink and the inedible pulp floats. Freezing the entire fruit also makes it easier to separate. Another very effective way of quickly harvesting the arils is to cut the pomegranate in half, score each half of the exterior rind four to six times, hold the pomegranate half over a bowl and smack the rind with a large spoon. The arils should eject from the pomegranate directly into the bowl, leaving only a dozen or more deeply embedded arils to remove.

The entire seed is consumed raw, though the watery, tasty aril is the desired part. The taste differs depending on the subspecies of pomegranate and its ripeness. The pomegranate juice can be very sweet or sour, but most fruits are moderate in taste, with sour notes from the acidic tannins contained in the aril juice. Pomegranate juice has long been a popular drink in Persian and Indian cuisine, and began to be widely distributed in the United States and Canada in 2002.

Grenadine syrup is thickened and sweetened pomegranate juice used in cocktail mixing. Before tomatoes (a New World fruit) arrived in the Middle East, grenadine was widely used in many Iranian foods, and is still found in traditional recipes such as *fesenjan*, a thick sauce made from pomegranate juice and ground walnuts, usually spooned over duck or other poultry and rice, and in *ash-e anar* (pomegranate soup).

Wild pomegranate seeds are used as a spice known as *anardana* (from Persian: *anar+dana, pomegranate+seed*), most notably in Indian and Pakistani cuisine, but also as a substitute for pomegranate syrup in Persian cuisine. Dried whole arils can often be obtained in ethnic Indian subcontinent markets. These seeds are separated from the flesh, dried for 10–15 days and used as an acidic agent for chutney and curry preparation. Ground *anardana* is also used, which results in a deeper flavoring in dishes and prevents the seeds from getting stuck in teeth. Seeds of the wild pomegranate variety known as *daru* from the Himalayas are regarded as quality sources for this spice.

Dried pomegranate arils, found in some natural specialty food markets, still contain the seed and residual aril water, maintaining a natural sweet and tart flavor. Dried arils can be used in several culinary applications, such as trail mix, granola bars, or as a topping for salad, yogurt, or ice cream. Chocolate covered arils, also available in gourmet food stores like Trader Joes, may be added to desserts and baked items.

In the Caucasus, pomegranate is used mainly as juice. In Azerbaijan a sauce from pomegranate juice (narsharab) is usually served with fish or tika kabab. In Turkey, pomegranate sauce, (Turkish: *nar eksisi*) is used as a salad dressing, to marinate meat, or simply to drink straight. Pomegranate seeds are also used in salads and sometimes as garnish for desserts such as güllaç. Pomegranate syrup or molasses is used in *muhammara*, a roasted red pepper, walnut, and garlic spread popular in Syria and Turkey.

In Greece, pomegranate is used in many recipes, including *kollivozoumi*, a creamy broth made from boiled wheat, pomegranates and raisins, legume salad with wheat and pomegranate, traditional Middle Eastern lamb kebabs with pomegranate glaze, pomegranate eggplant relish, and avocado-pomegranate dip. Pomegranate is also made into a liqueur and popular fruit confectionery used as ice cream topping or mixed with yogurt or spread as jam on toast. In Cyprus as well as in Greece and among the Greek Orthodox Diaspora, is used to make kolliva, a mixture of wheat, pomegranate seeds, sugar, almonds and other seeds served at memorial services.

In Ayurvedic Medicine

In the Indian subcontinent's ancient Ayurveda system of medicine, the pomegranate has extensively been used as a source of traditional remedies for thousands of years.

The rind of the fruit and the bark of the pomegranate tree is used as a traditional remedy against diarrhea, dysentery and intestinal parasites. The seeds and juice are considered a tonic for the heart and throat, and classified as a bitter-astringent (*pitta* or fire) component under the Ayurvedic system, and considered a healthful counterbalance to a diet high in sweet-fatty (*kapha* or earth) components. The astringent qualities of the flower juice, rind and tree bark are considered valuable for a variety of purposes, such as stopping nose bleeds and gum bleeds, toning skin, (after blending with mustard oil) firming-up sagging breasts and treating hemorrhoids. Pomegranate juice (of specific fruit strains) is also used as eyedrops as it is believed to slow the development of cataracts.

Ayurveda differentiates between pomegranate varieties and employs them for different remedies.

Pomegranate has been used as a contraceptive and abortifacient by means of consuming the seeds, or rind, as well as by using the rind as a vaginal suppository. This practice is recorded in ancient Indian literature, in Medieval sources, and in modern folk medicine.

Nutrients and Phytochemicals

Pomegranate aril juice provides about 16 per cent of an adult's daily vitamin C requirement per 100 ml serving, and is a good source of vitamin B_5 (pantothenic acid), potassium and natural phenols, such as ellagitannins and flavonoids. Pomegranates are listed as high-fibre in some charts of nutritional value. That fibre, however, is entirely contained in the edible seeds which also supply unsaturated oils. People who choose to discard the seeds forfeit nutritional benefits conveyed by the seed fibre, oils and micronutrients.

Phenolic Content

The most abundant polyphenols in pomegranate juice are the hydrolyzable tannins called ellagitannins formed when ellagic acid binds with a carbohydrate. Pomegranate ellagitannins, also called *punicalagins*, are tannins with free-radical scavenging properties in laboratory experiments and with potential human effects. Punicalagins are absorbed into the human body and may have dietary value as antioxidants, but conclusive proof of efficacy in humans has not yet been shown. During intestinal metabolism by bacteria, ellagitannins and punicalagins are converted to urolithins which have unknown biological activity *in vivo*. The different punicalagins present in *P. granatum* are granatin A and B, punicacortein A, B, C and D, 5-O-galloylpunicacortein D, punicafolin, punigluconin, punicalagin, 1-alpha-O-galloylpunicalagin, punicalin and 2-O-galloyl-punicalin. Other phenolics include catechins, gallocatechins, and anthocyanins, such as prodelphinidins, delphinidin, cyanidin, and pelargonidin. The ORAC (antioxidant capacity) of pomegranate juice was measured at 2,860 units per 100 grams. Many food and dietary supplement makers use pomegranate phenolic extracts as ingredients in their products instead of the juice. One of these extracts is ellagic acid, which may become bioavailable only after parent molecule punicalagins are metabolized. However, ingested ellagic acid from pomegranate juice does not accumulate in the blood in significant quantities and is rapidly excreted. Accordingly, ellagic acid from pomegranate juice does not appear to be biologically important *in vivo*

Potential Health Benefits

In preliminary laboratory research and clinical trials, juice of the pomegranate may be effective in reducing heart disease risk factors, including LDL oxidation, macrophage oxidative status, and foam cell formation. In an article published in the *American Journal of Clinical Nutrition* in 2000, researchers detailed an experiment in which healthy adult men and unhealthy mice consumed pomegranate juice daily. After two weeks, the healthy men experienced increased antioxidant levels, which resulted in a ninety percent drop in LDL cholestoral oxidation. In the mice, "oxidation of LDL by peritoneal macrophages was reduced by up to 90 per cent after pomegranate juice consumption".

In a limited study of hypertensive patients, consumption of pomegranate juice for two weeks was shown to reduce systolic blood pressure by inhibiting serum angiotensin-converting enzyme. Juice consumption may also inhibit viral infections while pomegranate extracts have antibacterial effects against dental plaque.

Despite limited research data, manufacturers and marketers of pomegranate juice have liberally used evolving research results for product promotion, especially for putative antioxidant health benefits. In February 2010, the FDA issued a Warning Letter to one such manufacturer, POM Wonderful, for using published literature to make illegal claims of unproven antioxidant and anti-disease benefits.

Pomelo

The pomelo (*Citrus maxima* or *Citrus grandis*) is a crisp citrus fruit native to South and Southeast Asia. It is usually pale green to yellow when ripe, with sweet white (or, more rarely, pink or red) flesh and very thick albedo (rind pith). It is the largest citrus fruit, 15-25 centimetres (5.9-9.8 in) in diameter, and usually weighing 1-2 kilograms (2.2-4.4 lb). Other spellings for pomelo include pummelo, and pommelo, and other names include Jeruk Bali, Chinese grapefruit, jabong, lusho fruit, pompelmous from Tamil *pampa limasu*, and shaddock.

The pomelo tastes like a sweet, mild grapefruit (which is itself a hybrid of the pomelo and the orange), though the typical pomelo is much larger in size than the grapefruit. It has very little, or none, of the common grapefruit's bitterness, but the enveloping membranous material around the segments is bitter, considered inedible, and thus usually is discarded. The peel is sometimes used to make marmalade, or is candied and sometimes dipped in chocolate. The peel of the pomelo 'Chandler', a California variety, has a smoother skin than many other varieties. An individual Chandler fruit can reach the weight of one kilogram. Pomelos are usually grafted onto other citrus rootstocks, but can be grown from seed, provided the seeds are not allowed to dry out before planting. The seedlings take about eight years to start blooming and yielding fruit.

The tangelo is a hybrid between the pomelo and the tangerine. It has a thicker skin than a tangerine and is less sweet. The orange is also suggested to be a hybrid of the two fruits. Mandelos are another pomelo hybrid.

The pomelo is native to Southeast Asia and is known there under a wide variety of names. In Vietnam, two particularly well-known varieties are cultivated; one called *bu i Nam Roi* in the Trà Ôn district of Vinh Long Province of the Mekong Delta region, and one called *bu?i da xanh* in Ben Tre Province.

In the Philippines, the fruit is known as the *sujâ*, or *lukban*, and is eaten as a dessert or snack. The pomelo, cut into wedges, is dipped in salt before it is eaten. The Philippine variety is usually red on the inside, and has more juice than other varieties, making it ideal for hiking. Pomelo juices and pomelo-flavored juice drink mixes are also common.

CHAPTER 16

Rambutan, Raisins

Rambutan

The rambutan is a medium-sized tropical tree in the family Sapindaceae. The fruit produced by the tree is also known as "rambutan." It is native to Vietnam, Indonesia, the Philippines, Sri Lanka, Malaysia, and elsewhere in Southeast Asia, although its precise natural distribution is unknown. It is closely related to several other edible tropical fruits including the lychee, longan and mamoncillo. It is believed to be native to the Malay Archipelago, from where it spread westwards to Thailand, Burma, Sri Lanka and India; eastwards to Vietnam, the Philippines and Indonesia. The name *rambutan* is derived from the Malay word *rambutan,* meaning "hairy". In Vietnam, it is called *chôm chôm* (meaning "messy hair") due to the spines covering the fruit's skin.

Rambutan fruit is naturally red in colour but they sometimes seem like yellow or orange. 'Rambut' is a malay word which means "hair", hence it got its name because of the Thorn like appearance. The shape of Rambutan fruit is round or oval and it is upto three to six to four cm in dimension. Rambutan is borne in clusters. Its leather like skin has flexible thorns. It has brownish seed with two to three cm in size and is basally scarred. It is soft and crusty.

Even though the raw seeds are poisonous, they may be eaten after cooking. Complete ripe fruits are mostly ugly brown in colour. The Rambutan tree grows upto 10 to 20 m in height. Its alternate leaves are 10 to 30 cm in length and have three to eleven leaflets, each and with an entire margin have a special structure. Small Flowers with leaf petal which are about 2 to 5 mm in size are in disk-shape and they have bloomed cluster wise.

Taste: A good rambutan has a firm and juicy flesh. It has a sweat taste, and it is somewhat similar taste of lychee fruit. The tree will actually look like a enlarged Christmas tree. A rambutan is best within mid-season somewhere around June-August as they seem to be most sweet, and large. It is more sweet than sour. When it gets ripened the flesh separates easily from the seed. But when it is not quite ripe, the flesh sticks to the rambutan seed and the taste is a little sour overall, still not a bad taste though.

A second species regularly sold in Costa Rican markets is often known as "wild" rambutan. Yellow in colour, it is a little smaller than the usual red variety. The flesh exposed when the outer skin is peeled off is sweet and sour, slightly grape-like and gummy to the taste. In Costa Rican Spanish, it is known as *mamón chino* (literally translated as "Chinese sucker") due to its Asian origin and the likeness of the edible part with *Melicoccus bijugatus*.

Rambutan are non-climacteric fruit - that is, they ripen only on the tree.

It is a popular garden fruit tree and propagated commercially in small orchards. It is one of the best known fruits of Southeast Asia and is also widely cultivated elsewhere in the tropics including Africa, the Caribbean islands, Costa Rica, Panama, India, Indonesia, the Philippines, and Sri Lanka. Thailand is the largest producer from Surat Thani Province Thailand. Rambutan production is increasing in Australia and, in 1997, was one of the top three tropical fruits produced in Hawaii. It is also produced in Ecuador where it is known as "achotillo" and on the island of Puerto Rico.

The fruit are usually sold fresh, used in making jams and jellies, or canned. Evergreen rambutan trees with their abundant coloured fruit make beautiful landscape specimens.

The best quality rambutan is generally that which is harvested still attached to the branch. It is less susceptible to rot, damage, and pests, and remains fresh for a much longer time than rambutan that has been picked from the branch.

Another indicator of quality is the ease of detachment of the flesh from the seed. An easily detachable flesh normally will have bits of the woody seed coating. Thus, it is a common Malay wisdom to not eat too much rambutan when one has a cough.

Nutritional Value per Serving

Rambutan, canned, syrup pack Nutritional value per serving Serving size 100 g Energy 343 kJ (82 kcal) Carbohydrates 20.87 - Dietary fibre 0.9 Fat 0.21 Protein 0.65 Water 78.04 g Vitamin A equiv. 0 μg (0%) Vitamin A 3 IU - beta-carotene 2 μg (0%) Thiamine (vit. B_1) 0.013 mg (1%) Riboflavin (vit. B_2) 0.022 mg (2%) Niacin (vit. B_3) 1.352 mg (9%) Pantothenic acid (B_5) 0.018 mg (0%) Vitamin B_6 0.020 mg (2%) Folate (vit. B_9) 8 μg (2%) Vitamin B_{12} 0.00 μg (0%) Vitamin C 4.9 mg (6%) Calcium 22 mg (2%) Iron 0.35 mg (3%) Magnesium 7 mg (2%) Manganese 0.343 mg (16%) Phosphorus 9 mg (1%) Potassium 42 mg (1%) Sodium 10.9 mg (1%).

Rambutan is a juicy fruit and it is very popular and tasty fruit in many countries. Seed oil from the Rambutan is formed and is used to manufacture candles and soap. Although Rambutan trees are not cut down often. This wood is also used in the construction industry. Rambutan fruit is said to heal dysentery and diarrhea effectively. This fruit leaves are also used as cataplasm to cure headaches. In Malaysia, Rambutan fruit skin is used to prepare native medicines. Further, Rambutan trees roots are boiled and used as a medication to cure fever.

Cultivated for its fresh fruit, it is also made as syrup and cooked for stewed fruit and jams. The colourful fruits are regularly used in displays with flower and fruit arrangements. Young shoots are used to produce a green colour on silk that is first dyed yellow with turmeric. The fruit dye is one of the ingredients to dye silk a black colour. The seeds are edible when roasted, they are bitter and said to be narcotic.

Nutritional Value: It is a good source of vitamin C and calcium, rambutan fruit provides fairly a good amount of niacin, iron, protein and fibre. A recent study found out that eating nine to ten fruits and vegetables of rambutan family per day, were effective in lowering blood pressure.

Health Benefits of Rambutan

Rambutan fruit contains carbohydrate, protein, fat, phosphorus, iron, calcium and vitamin C. Coat tannin of fruit and Leaves contain saponin. The seeds always contain fat and polifenol. Skin and stem contains tannin, saponin, flavonida, pectic substances, and iron. Rambutans roots, bark and leaves have various uses in the production of dyes and drugs. Part of this plant can be used as a medicinal fruit and have benefits for health such as:

- *Reduce Body Fat*
- *Make skin softer*
- *Hair care*
- *Treat dysentery*
- *Treat diabetes*

Raisins

Raisins are known as dried grapes. Raisins may be eaten raw or used in cooking, baking and brewing. In the United Kingdom, Ireland, Australia, and Canada the word "raisin" is reserved for the dried large dark grape, with "sultana" being a dried large white grape, and "currant" being a dried small Black Corinth grape. The health benefits of this fruit include relief from constipation, acidosis, anemia, fever, and sexual weakness. Raisins also help in weight gain, eye care, dental care, and bone health.

Nutritive Value per 100 g of Rambutan

Principle	Nutritive Value
Protein	1.0 g
Cholesterol	0.0 mg
Thiamin	0.01mg
Vitamin C	7.4 mg
Sodium	16.5 mg
Potassium	63.0 mg
Calcium	33.0 mg
Vitamin A	4.5 IU
Iron	0.5 mg

Person Whom May Consume Raisins

Mouth Problem

Raisins contain oleanolic acid that provides protection against cavities and tooth decay, and also prevents the growth of harmful bacteria that can cause gingivitis and other periodontal diseases. So person who intake raisins will get relieve from tooth pain.

Bone Problem

Raisins are rich in calcium are necessary to strengthen bones and teeth. A micronutrient known as boron are abundant in this fruit aids calcium absorption and bone formation. If you are a postmenopausal woman, raisins are a good snack for you because the calcium and boron present in them helps to prevent the development of osteoporosis. The potassium and magnesium contents of raisins help reduce acidity (an abnormal metabolic condition known as acidosis) and remove toxins from the body, which may cause diseases such as arthritis, gout, kidney stones and heart disease.

Eye Care

Raisins are rich in calcium are necessary to strengthen bones and teeth. A micronutrient known as boron are abundant in this fruit aids calcium absorption and bone formation. If you are a postmenopausal woman, raisins are a good snack for you because the calcium and boron present in them helps to prevent the development of osteoporosis. The potassium and magnesium contents of raisins help reduce acidity (an abnormal metabolic condition known as acidosis) and remove toxins from the body, which may cause diseases such as arthritis, gout, kidney stones and heart disease.

Cancer

The polyphenolic antioxidant present in raisins, known as catechin, provides protection against free radicals, which causes the development of tumors, specifically colon cancer.

Anemia

It is caused by decrease in the number of red blood cells in the body. Raisins contain considerable amount of iron which directly helps treating anemia. It also contains many members of vitamin-B complex which are essential for formation of blood. Copper in them also help formation of red blood cells. So, if you notice any decrease in the hemoglobin level in your blood, eat more raisins to raise it. Raisins also help to correct iron deficiency anemia and promote blood clotting during wound healing.

Constipation

Raisins swell as the fibre present in them in dried form absorbs water, when person feel in time of indigestion. This helps giving relief in constipation.

CHAPTER 17

Manilkara Zapota (*Chiku*)

Manilkara Zapota, commonly known as the sapodilla, is a long-lived, evergreen tree native to southern Mexico, Central America and the Caribbean. An example natural occurrence is in coastal Yucatan in the Petenes mangroves ecoregion, where it is a subdominant plant species. It was introduced to the Philippines during Spanish colonization. It is grown in huge quantities in India, Pakistan and Mexico. It is also known as *Chikoo/Chiku* in northern India and Pakistan and *Sapota* in some parts of South India.

Sapodilla can grow to more than 30 m (98 ft) tall with an average trunk diametre of 1.5 m (4.9 ft). The average height of cultivated specimens, however, is usually between 9 and 15 m (30 and 49 ft) with a trunk diameter not exceeding 50 cm (20 in). It is wind-resistant and the bark is rich in a white, gummy latex called chicle. The ornamental leaves are medium green and glossy. They are alternate, elliptic to ovate, 7-15 cm long, with an entire margin. The white flowers are inconspicuous and bell-like, with a six-lobed corolla.

The fruit is a large ellipsoid berry, 4-8 cm in diameter, very much resembling a smooth-skinned potato and containing two to five seeds. Inside, its flesh ranges from a pale yellow to an earthy brown colour with a grainy texture akin to that of a well-ripened pear. The seeds are black and resemble beans, with a hook at one end that can catch in the throat if swallowed. The fruit has a high latex content and does not ripen until picked, whereupon the fruit softens to a firmness and appearance very similar to that of a fuzzy, brown-skinned kiwifruit.

The fruit has an exceptionally sweet, malty flavor. Many believe the flavour bears a striking resemblance to caramel or a pear candied with brown sugar. The unripe fruit is hard to the touch and contains high amounts of saponin, which has astringent properties similar to tannin, drying out the mouth.

The trees can only survive in warm, typically tropical environments, dying easily if the temperature drops below freezing. From germination, the sapodilla tree will usually take anywhere from five to eight years to bear fruit. The sapodilla trees yield fruit twice a year, though flowering may continue year round.

Scientific classification Kingdom: Plantae (unranked): Angiosperms (unranked): Eudicots (unranked): Asterids Order: Ericales Family: Sapotaceae Genus: *Manilkara* Species: *M. zapota.*

Synonyms

- *Achradelpha mammosa* O.F. Cook
- *Achras mammosa* L.
- *Achras zapota* L.
- *Achras zapotilla* (Jacq.) Nutt.
- *Calocarpum mammosum* Pierre
- *Lucuma mammosa* C.F.Gaertn.
- *Manilkara achras* Mill. (Fosberg)
- *Manilkara zapotilla* (Jacq.) Gilly
- *Pouteria mammosa* Cronquist
- *Sapota zapotilla* (Jacq.) Coville

Other Names

Sapodilla is known as *sapodilla* in Guyana, Grenada, and Trinidad & Tobago, *zapote* in Colombia, Honduras, El Salvador,

Cuba, and the Dominican Republic, *níspero* in Costa Rica, Cuba, Puerto Rico, Nicaragua, and Venezuela, *dilly* in the Bahamas, *naseberry* in Jamaica and other parts of the Caribbean, *sapoti* in Brazil and Haiti, *chico* or *tsiko* in the Philippines and *chicosapote* or *chicozapote* in Mexico, Hawaii, southern California and southern Florida.

It is called *ciku* in standard Malay and *sawo nilo* in Kelantanese Malay. In Chinese, the name is mistakenly translated by many people roughly as "ginseng fruit", though this is also the name used for the pepino, an unrelated fruit; it should instead be "heart fruit" because it is shaped like the heart.

CHAPTER 18

Tomatoes, Tamarillo

Tomatoes

Presently, tomatoes are one of the most famous vegetables eaten by Americans. Tomatoes are members of the fruit family, but they are served and prepared as a vegetable and so most people consider them a vegetable and not a fruit. Tomatoes are a great source of vitamin C and also a good source of vitamin A.

There are thousands of tomato varieties. The most commonly available varieties are: cherry, plum, and slicing tomatoes. A new sweet variety which is like the cherry tomato is the grape tomato; it is tasty to eat alone or in a salad.

Cold temperatures spoil tomatoes, so do not buy tomatoes that are stored in a cold area. Choose plump tomatoes with smooth skins that have no bruises, cracks, or blemishes. Depending on the variety, ripe tomatoes will be completely red or reddish-orange. Storage: Tomatoes should be stored at room temperature (above 55 degrees) until they have fully ripened. This will allow them to ripen well and develop good flavor and aroma. Do not store tomatoes in direct sunlight, because sunlight will cause them to ripen irregularly. If you must store them for a longer period of time, store them in the refrigerator and serve them at room temperature. Sliced tomatoes can be frozen for use in sauces or other cooked dishes.

- Tomatoes are needed for tossed salads.
- Tomatoes can be used in hot or cold dishes.
- Place tomatoes stem-up, to avoid bruising the shoulders.
- Look for well-formed tomatoes which are smooth, ripe and blemish-free.

Tomatoes are obtainable much of the year, from mid-May through mid-November. Tomatoes are grown in southwest Georgia and it is one of the state's top cash crops.

Tamarillo

Solanum betaceum (syn. Cyphomandra betacea) is a small tree or shrub in the flowering plant family Solanaceae. It is best known as the species that bears the tamarillo, an egg-shaped edible fruit. Other names include tree tomato and tomate de árbol.

The fruits are egg shaped and about 4-10 centimeters long. Their colour varies from yellow and orange to red and almost purple. Sometimes they have dark, longitudinal stripes. Red fruits are more acetous, yellow and orange fruits are sweeter. The flesh has a firm texture and contains more and larger seeds than a common tomato. The fruits are very high in vitamin and iron and low in calories (only about 40 calories per fruit).

The fruit is eaten by scooping the flesh from a halved fruit. When lightly sugared and cooled, the flesh is used for a breakfast dish. Yellow-fruited cultivars have a sweeter flavor, occasionally compared to mango or apricot. The red-fruited variety, which is much more widely cultivated is more tart, and the savory aftertaste is far more pronounced. In the Northern Hemisphere, tamarillos are most frequently available from July until November, and fruits early in the season tend to be sweeter and less astringent.

They can be made into compotes, or added to stews (e.g. Boeuf Bourguignon), hollandaise, chutneys and curries. Desserts using this fruit include bavarois and, combined with apples, a strudel.

In Colombia, Ecuador, Panama and parts of Indonesia (including Sumatra and Sulawesi), fresh tamarillos are frequently blended together with water and sugar to make a juice. It is also available as a commercially pasteurized purée. In Nepal it is grown in the hill parts/mountains. it is yellow in colour and used as Pickle or chutney and used as Tomato for Curry. it is known in Nepal As ram bheda, rukh (tree) bheda, or tree tomato.

The flesh of the tamarillo is tangy and variably sweet, with a bold and complex flavour, and may be compared to kiwifruit, tomato, guava, or passion fruit. The skin and the flesh near it have a bitter taste and are not usually eaten raw.

Research and breeding should improve plantation management, fruit quality and postharvest treatment. A better understanding of plant physiology, nutritional requirements of plants and fruit set mechanisms will help to improve growing systems. Breeding goals are to break seed dormancy, to improve sweetness of fruits and to increase yield. For industrial uses, little "stones" of sodium and calcium that occasionally appear in the fruit skin form a problem. Those stones have to be eliminated by breeding.

CHAPTER 19

Watermelon, Walnuts

Watermelon

Watermelon (*Citrullus lanatus* (Thunb), family Cucurbitaceae) is a vine-like (scrambler and trailer) flowering plant originally from southern Africa. Its fruit, which is also called *watermelon*, is a special kind referred to by botanists as a pepo, a berry which has a thick rind (exocarp) and fleshy centre (mesocarp and endocarp). Pepos are derived from an inferior ovary, and are characteristic of the Cucurbitaceae. The watermelon fruit, loosely considered a type of melon – although not in the genus *Cucumis* – has a smooth exterior rind (green, yellow and sometimes white) and a juicy, sweet interior flesh (usually deep red to pink, but sometimes orange, yellow and even green if not ripe). It is also commonly used to make a variety of salads, most notably fruit salad.

A watermelon contains about 6 per cent sugar and 92 per cent water by weight. As with many other fruits, it is a source of vitamin C.

The amino-acid citrulline was first extracted from watermelon and analyzed. Watermelons contain a significant amount of citrulline and after consumption of several kg, an elevated concentration is measured in the blood plasma; this could be mistaken for citrullinaemia or other urea cycle disorders.

Watermelon rinds, usually a light green or white colour, are also edible and contain many hidden nutrients, but most people avoid eating them due to their unappealing flavor. They are sometimes used as a vegetable. In China, they are stir-fried, stewed or more often pickled. When stir-fried, the de-skinned and de-fruited rind is cooked with olive oil, garlic, chili peppers, scallions, sugar and rum. Pickled watermelon rind is also commonly consumed in the Southern US. Watermelon juice can be made into wine.

Watermelon is mildly diuretic and contains large amounts of beta carotene. Watermelon with red flesh is a significant source of lycopene.

There are more than 1200 varieties of watermelon, ranging in weight from less than a pound to more than two hundred pounds, with flesh that is red, orange, yellow or white.

The Carolina Cross produced the current world record watermelon weighing 262 pounds (119 kg). It has green skin, red flesh and commonly produces fruit between 65 and 150 pounds (29 and 68 kg). It takes about 90 days from planting to harvest.

The Yellow Crimson has a yellow coloured flesh. It has been described as sweeter and more honey-flavored than the more popular red flesh watermelon.

The Orangeglo has a very sweet orange pulp, and is a large oblong fruit weighing 9-14 kg (20-30 pounds). It has a light green rind with jagged dark green stripes. It takes about 90-100 days from planting to harvest.

The Moon and Stars variety was created in 1926. The rind is purple/black and has many small yellow circles (stars) and one or two large yellow circles (moon). The melon weighs 9-23 kg (20-50 pounds). The flesh is pink or red and has brown seeds. The foliage is also spotted. The time from planting to harvest is about 90 days.

The Cream of Saskatchewan consists of small round fruits around 25 cm (10 inches) in diameter. It has a quite thin, light green with dark green striped rind, with sweet white flesh and black seeds. It can grow well in cool climates. It was originally brought to Saskatchewan, Canada, by Russian immigrants. The melon takes 80-85 days from planting to harvest.

The Melitopolski has small round fruits roughly 28-30 cm (11-12 inches) in diametre. It is an early ripening variety that originated from the Volga River region of Russia, an area known for cultivation of watermelons. The Melitopolski watermelons are seen piled high by vendors in Moscow in summer. This variety takes around 95 days from planting to harvest.

The Densuke watermelon has round fruit up to 25 lb (11 kg). The rind is black with no stripes or spots. It is grown only on the island of Hokkaido, Japan, where up to 10,000 watermelons are produced every year. In June 2008, one of the first harvested watermelons was sold at an auction for 650,000 yen (6,300 USD), making the most expensive watermelon ever sold. The average selling price is generally around 25,000 yen.

Nutritional value per 100 g (3.5 oz) Energy 127 kJ (30 kcal) Carbohydrates 7.55 g - Sugars 6.2 g - Dietary fibre 0.4 g Fat 0.15 g Protein 0.61 g Water 91.45 g Vitamin A equiv. 28 µg (4%) Thiamine (vit. B1) 0.033 mg (3%) Riboflavin (vit. B2) 0.021 mg (2%) Niacin (vit. B3) 0.178 mg (1%) Pantothenic acid (B5) 0.221 mg (4%) Vitamin B6 0.045 mg (3%) Folate (vit. B9) 3 µg (1%) Vitamin C 8.1 mg (10%) Calcium 7 mg (1%) Iron 0.24 mg (2%) Magnesium 10 mg (3%) Phosphorus 11 mg (2%) Potassium 112 mg (2%) Zinc 0.10 mg (1%).

Watermelon is an American preferred for meals and snacks. People can't get sufficient of the sweet treat, and nutritionists have long appreciated the health benefits watermelon provides. In recent research new light is found on its potential health benefits. Watermelon contains more lycopene, an antioxidant that may help to reduce the risks of cancer and other diseases.

Watermelon, the fruit which is really a Vegetable. Watermelon can be traced back to Africa and it is part of the cucumber and squash family. Early watermelons were mostly rind and seeds. Today's varieties are larger, the flesh is sweeter, the seeds are smaller and the rind is thinner. It is the most refreshing, thirst satisfying fruit of all. It consists of 92 per cent water and 8 per cent sugar, so it is appropriately named. Americans consume over 17 lbs of watermelon each year. The largest watermelon on world record (Guinness Book of World Records) weights 262 pounds.

Watermelons are mostly available throughout year. It is a perfect fruit to a salad, salsa, or cool drink. There are over 50 varieties of watermelon. Most of it have reddish flesh, but there are orange and yellow-fleshed varieties also. Among the 50 varieties of watermelon, common in the United States are: Allsweet, Ice-Box, Seedless and Yellow Flesh.

If picked earlier, watermelon will not ripen easily. If unripe, try putting the melon in a paper bag with un-refrigerated; this may sometimes works to ripen them. Watermelons can be preserved for short period of time, up to 2 weeks, uncut at room temperature. Wash watermelon with soap and water before cutting and once cut, pack the uneaten in closed plastic containers or bags and put back in the refrigerator.

Selecting Watermelon

Unlike other melon-types watermelon can't be chosen from its smell. The only way to pick a ripe watermelon at your store is to do the flat hand test: Tap the melon with flat hand. If the sound is deep and thick you probably have found a ripe and sweet fruit.

Walnuts

If you are going a little more towards nuts, doesn't matter. You can now have a handful of walnuts and enjoy them after a heavy fat meal. Walnuts, a rich source of the omega-3 fat improve the artery function after a fat meal. New research shows that eating a handful of raw walnuts along with meals high in saturated fat appears to limit the possibility of the harmful fat to damage arteries.

"People would get the wrong message if they think that they can continue eating unhealthy fats provided they add walnuts to their meals," said researchers where the research was conducted. "Instead, they should consider making walnuts part of a healthy diet that limits saturated fats.

Walnut provides vascular protection. It helps to decrease the sudden onset of inflammation and oxidation in the arteries.

Walnut as a better food ? Walnuts are often known as a "brain food," not only because of the wrinkled brain-like appearance of their shells, but since they high concentration of omega-3 fats. For your brain cells to function properly, this structural fat needs to be primarily the omega-3 fats found in walnuts and cold-water fish.

The cell membranes of our body including the neurons in our brain are composed of fats. They are the gate keepers to allow certain things and disallow others into the cell. Omega 3 is especially a fluid which makes the whole process a lot easier, thus maximized the cells ability to promote nutrients and eliminating wastes, a good way to keep them away.

Bibliography

Burkill, I.H. (1931). An Enumeration of the Species of Paramignya, Atalantia and Citrus, Found in Malaya. *Gard. Bull. Straits Settlem*. 5: 212-220.

Creasy, G.L./Creasy, L.L. (2009). *Grapes* (Crop Production Science in Horticulture). CABI.

Denham, T., Haberle, S.G., Lentfer, C., Fullagar, R., Field, J., Porch, N., Therin, M., Winsborough B., and Golson, J. "Multi-disciplinary Evidence for the Origins of Agriculture from 6950-6440 Cal BP at Kuk Swamp in the Highlands of New Guinea." *Science*, June 2003 Issue.

Editors (2006). "Banana fibre rugs". *Dwell* 6 (7): 44. Brief Mention of Banana Fibre Rugs.

Ensminger, Audrey H.; *et al.* (1995). *The Concise Encyclopedia of Foods & Nutrition*. CRC Press. p. 651.

Gulsen, O.; M.L. Roose (2001). "Lemons: Diversity and Relationships with Selected *Citrus* Genotypes as Measured with Nuclear Genome Markers". *Journal of the American Society of Horticultural Science*, 126: 309-317.

Gutiérrez, R.M.; Mitchell, S. & Solis, R.V. (2008): *Psidium guajava*: A Review of its Traditional Uses, Phytochemistry and Pharmacology. *J. Ethnopharmacol.* 117(1): 1-27.

Leibling, Robert W. and Pepperdine, Donna (2006). "Natural Remedies of Arabia". *Saudi Aramco World* 57 (5): 14. Banana Etymology, Banana Flour.

Litz, Richard E. (Editor, 2009). *The Mango: Botany, Production and Uses*. 2nd Edition. CABI.

Mabberley, D.J. (1998). Australian Citreae with Notes on Other Aurantioideae (Rutaceae).

Morton, J. 1987. Sapodilla. p. 393-398. In: Fruits of Warm Climates. Julia F. Morton, Miami, FL.

Ojewole, J.A. (2006): Antiinflammatory and Analgesic Effects of *Psidium guajava* Linn. (Myrtaceae) Leaf Aqueous Extract in Rats and Mice. *Methods and Findings in Experimental and Clinical Pharmacology* 28(7): 441-446.

Skidmore, T., Smith, P. – *Modern Latin America* (5th Edition), (2001) New York: Oxford University Press.

Watson, Andrew. *Agricultural Innovation in the Early Islamic World*, New York: Cambridge University Press, 1983.

Index

A

Acai, 19
- acai berry facts, 21-22
- acai health benefits, 20-21

AIDS, 24

Almond, 24

Alzheimer, 21

Andhra Pradesh, 48

Apple, 11, 18

Apricot, 22
- benefits of apricot, 22
  - anemia, 22
  - constipation, 22-23
  - digestion, 23
  - eyes/vision, 23
  - fever, 23
  - skin disease, 23-24
- person whom may not consume apricot, 24
  - asthma problem, 24
  - diarrhea, 24
  - kidney stones, 24
  - respiratory disease, 24

ARMD, 159

ASEAN, 66

Avocado, 25
- anti-cancer benefits, 30-31
- health benefits, 25
- optimized absorption of cartenoids, 27-28
- promotes blood sugar regulation, 29-30
- supports cardiovascular health, 28-29
- wide-ranging anti-inflammatory benefits, 27

B

Banana Pancake Trail, 48

Banana, 40-50
- Cavendish, 45-46
- flower, 48
- leaves, 48-49
- nutrition and research, 49
- other uses, 49-50
- storage and transport, 46-48
- trunk, 49

Bananas, 12

Bangladesh, 91

Berry fruits, 32-39
- barberries, 36
- bilberry, 33
- blueberry, 33-34
- cloudberry, 32-33
- consume of cranberries, 37
  - bacterial disease, 37-38

cancer and heart attack, 38
gallstone, 38
cranberry, 37
gooseberry, 34
huckleberry, 36
mulberry, 34-35
nannyberry, 37
person whom may not consume
cranberries, 38
blood thinners, 38-39
raspberry, 35
wineberry, 35-36
Black Monukka, 78
Buddhist forest, 92

C

C. maxima, 82
Carbon dioxide, 47
Carcinogenic Potency Project, 138
Caribbean islands, 177
Centres for Disease Control and Prevention, 1992, 5
Cerasus, 52
Chekiang Provinces of China, 96
Cherries, 12
Cherry, 52-56
Cherry Marketing Institute, 55
China, 18
Chlorophyll, 46
Christian religion, 61
Christmas tree, 177
Citrus fruits, 10
Citrus japonica, 94
Citrus reticulata, 122
Citrus sinensis, 93
Clementines, 51-52
Concord grapes, 79
Costa Rica, 143

D

D. dulcis, 64
Date palm leaves, 61
Date palm wood, 61
Durian, 62-67
Dates, 12, 58-70
De Agri Cultura, 73
Different kinds of fruits source of vitamins, 11-17
Diospyros, 160
DNA, 4
Dominician Republic, 184
Dried grapes, 82
Durian, 12, 62-67
Durio zibethinus, 63

E

Edible fig, 73
Einset seedless, 78
Ericaceae, 36
Eutere oleracea, 19

F

Figs plants, 72
Figs, 71-75
colon cancer, 74
coronary heart disease, 74
diabetes, 75
hypertension, 75
lower cholesterol, 74
menopausal breast cancer, 75
piles, 75
sexual weakness, 75
weight loss, 74

Fruits, 1

G

GABA, 133

Golden Passion Fruit, 143

Grapes, grape fruit, guava fruit, 13, 76-88

grape, 13, 76-79

benefits, 80-82

seed constituents, 79-80

grapefruit, 82-85

nutritional information, 85-86

guava fruit, 86-88

potential medical uses, 88

Guidelines for Voluntary Nutrition Labeling of Raw Fruits, Vegetables and Fish, 158

Guineo Verde, 46

Gulf of Mexico, 77

H

Hortus malabaricus, 89

I

Introduction, 1-10

asthma, 9

bone metabolism and osteoporosis, 8

cognitive function, 8

factors affecting citrus consumption, 9

kidney stone disease, 8

nutrient content and functions of citrus, 2-3

carbohydrate, 3

folate, 4-5

phytochemicals, 5

phytochemicals in citrus fruits, 5

potassium, 5

vitamin C, 3-4

nutritional and health benefits of citrus fruits, 2

prevention potential of citrus, 6

anaemia, 7

cancer, 6-7

cardiovascular disease, 6

cataracts, 7-8

neural tube defects, 7

J

Jackfruit, 13, 89-92

Jordan valley, 73

K

Kiwifruit, 99

age related muscular degeneration, 102

cardiovascular disease, 102

constipation, 103

heart and colon health, 101

Kordia, 57

Kumquat, 13

characteristics, 94-95

cultivation, 95

Hong Kong or chin chu, 96-97

Jiangsu kumquat, 95-96

Marumi or round kumquat, 97

Meiwa or large round kumquat, 97

Nagami or oval kumquat, 98-99

Nordmann seedless kumquat, 98

oval kumquat, 94

round kumquat, 94

L

LDL, 80
Leathery berry, 42
Lemon, 104
Lemon, lime, lychee, 104-121
  differences between orange and lemon, 106
  growing lemons, 105
  non-culinary uses, 108-110
  person whom may consume lemon, 110-112
  varieties, 106-108
Lime, 112
  health effects, 113
  person whom may consume lime, 113
LLC, 26
London Horticultural Society, 93
Low-density lipoprotein (LDL), 6
Lychee, 14, 116

M

Malabar Coast, 89
Malus domestica, 18
Mandarin, 122
Mandarin, mango purple mangosteen, mulberry, 14, 122-135
Mangifera indica, 124
Mango, 124
  body immunity, 129
  brain health, 129
  cancer hazards and lower cholesterol, 128
  cures acne, 128
  cures anemia and helps in pregnancy, 128
  digestion, 128
  rheumatism, 129
  scurvy, 129
Mangosteen, 14
Manilkara zapota, 182-184
  other names, 183-184
  synonyms, 183
Musa acuminata, 40, 43
Musa balbisiana, 40, 43
Musa paradisiaca, 40, 43

N

National Health and Nutrition Examination Study, 26
Nectarine, 14
Nepal, 91
Northern Highbush Blueberry, 33
NSP, 3
Nutrition Impact, 26

O

Olive, 139
  bone health, 141-142
  person whom may consume olive, 140-141
ORAC, 173
Orange, 136
  olive, 136-142
  products made from oranges, 137-139

P

P. prostrate, 52
Papaya, 147
Passionfruit, 15, 143-175
  nutritional value per 100 g, 146-147
Peaches, 153

health benefits of peaches, 154-155

Pear, 143-175

health benefits, 157-159

person whom may consume pear, 159-160

Persea Americana, 25

Persimmon, 15, 160

Pineapple, 163

person whom may consume pineapple, 165-166

Plant Sterols, 20

Plum, 15, 166

Pomegranate, 169

ayurvedic medicine, 171-174

Pomelo, 174

Prunus armeniaca, 22

Prunus avium, 52

Purple mangosteen, 130

mulberry, 132

pain, 134

person whom may consume mulberry, 133-134

person whom may not consume mulberry, 134-135

uses in folk medicine, 132

R

Raisins, 179

Rambutan, 16, 176

health benefits of rambutan, 179

nutritional value per serving, 178-179

person whom may consume raisins, 180-181

Red Blood Cells (RBCs), 22

RNA, 4

Rome by Lucius Licinius Lucullus, 55

Royal Botanic Gardens, 66

Russian seedless, 78

S

Sapodillas, 16

Star apple, 16

Stripped fruit, 61

T

Tamarillo, 186

TB, 24

Thompson seedless, 78

Tijuca Forest area, 90

Tamarillo, 185-187

Tomatoes, 185

U

UNESCO, 61

United States, 18

University of Florida, 21

US Department of Agriculture in 1910-1912, 97

US Ruby Red, 1929, 83

USDA, 73

V

V. corymbosum, 33

Vaazhai-ch-charugu, 49

Vaccinium uliginosum, 33

Vitis labrusca, 76

Vitis vinifera, 76

W

Walnuts, 191

Watermelon, 17, 188